NICOLA MAGRIN—*By Dint of Being Wind,* watercolor on paper, 2018

Without
Ever
Reaching
the
Summit

Without Ever Reaching the Summit

a journey

PAOLO COGNETTI

Translated from the Italian by Stash Luczkiw

HarperOne
An Imprint of HarperCollinsPublishers

HarperCollins books may be purchased for educational, business, or
sales promotional use. For information, please email the Special Markets
Department at SPsales@harpercollins.com.

Originally published as *Senza mai arrivare in cima* in Italy in 2018 by
Einaudi.

FIRST EDITION

Designed by Terry McGrath
Illustration on frontispiece by Nicola Magrin; used by permission.
All other art by Paolo Cognetti.

Library of Congress Cataloging-in-Publication Data is available upon
request.

ISBN 978-0-06-297831-8

20 21 22 23 24   LSC   10 9 8 7 6 5 4 3 2 1

I'd like to be a painter
more than a wordsmith
this morning.
The giant rhododendrons
stand out in the fog
with their big mossy hugs.

Tiziano Terzani, *An Idea of Destiny*

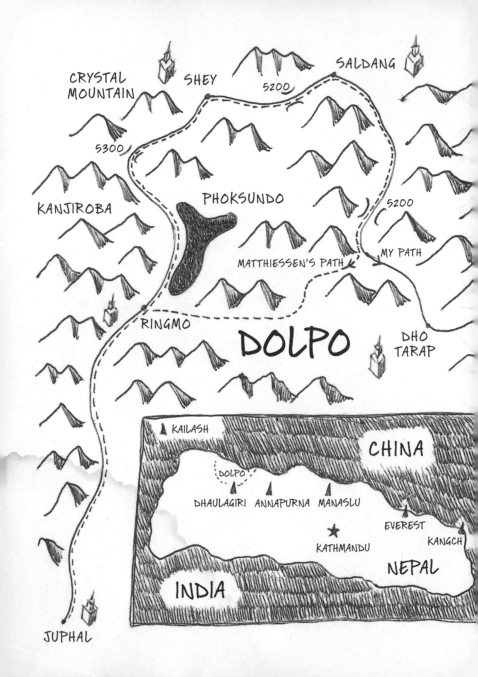

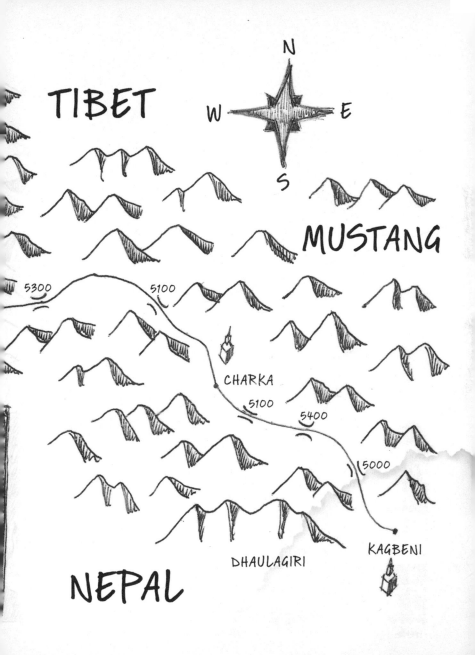

Contents

Introduction

Toward the end of 2017, and my fortieth year of life, I left with some companions for the land of Dolpo, a plateau in northwestern Nepal where we would go over passes at altitudes of more than five thousand meters, trekking for about a month along the Tibetan border. Tibet was a destination that couldn't be reached, and not because of border issues: invaded by the Chinese army in 1950, devastated in the sixties and seventies by the Cultural Revolution's fury, then inexorably colonized by the new capitalist

China, that ancient kingdom of monks, merchants, and nomadic shepherds simply no longer exists.

But I was told that there was a little Tibet in Nepalese territory. It had survived somehow thanks to history's forgetfulness. Even on maps Dolpo looks like an anomaly: where Nepal's political borders, which normally remain south of the Himalayan chain, extend beyond it and penetrate the immense geographical area of the Tibetan plateau, there is a whole region above four thousand meters untouched by the monsoons or paved roads—the most arid, remote, and least populated part of the country. *Perhaps up there,* I said to myself, *I could see the Tibet that no longer exists, that none of us can see anymore.* This was the journey I wanted for my fortieth birthday, a fitting way to celebrate my farewell to that other lost kingdom: youth.

It wasn't the only motive for going. One equally important was the caravan I would be part of. The Himalayas are not to be taken lightly; to travel hundreds of kilometers among uninhabited mountains a real expedition is needed, with guides, porters, mules, a camp to assemble every evening and dismantle every morning, and fellow travelers.

Of the nine who left with me, one was Nicola, with whom there was a bond of nascent friendship. We had just met, we felt like we were alike, and we were in that phase in which we had everything to discover about each other. But we both believed that you don't just watch friendships happen; they have to be built with a foundation, they need memorable endeavors for the future. So one spring day I described Dolpo on the phone to him and asked, "Do you want to go together?"

"Yes," he responded.

By now it was autumn and neither of us had turned back.

The other companion was Remigio, my dearest and most difficult friend at that point in my life. In the ten years of our friendship I was never able to take him away from the mountain village where he had been born and raised, and where I had gone to live. Not that I wanted to uproot him. I just wanted to share something different with him: a place where we were both foreigners, a sense of remoteness and exploration. I worked on him shoulder to shoulder for months, used every possible technique of persuasion, and all I got were doubts and second thoughts. He always had a bum knee, or was short on money, or his car was breaking down. Eventually he showed up at the airport just when I was resigned to not seeing him.

"So you're coming too?" I asked.

"Well, yeah," he replied, shrugging his shoulders.

I knew that in the mountains you walk alone even when walking with someone, but I was happy to share my solitude with these companions.

We left in early October, when snow was already expected in the Alps, and we landed in a hot and dusty Kathmandu, fresh out of the monsoon season. Since my last visit, the city seemed to have expanded into its wide valley: there were further layers of suburbs, slums, residential neighborhoods, stray dogs, monkeys, beggars, skeletal cows in the middle of the road, children. The

Hindu and Buddhist temples in Durbar Square had been damaged or completely destroyed by the earthquake two years before, with rubble strewn around the wooden struts holding up the walls that were still standing. Large billboards announced that the Chinese government was taking care of the reconstruction. China? What was China doing in Nepal's most important square?

From home I had brought a fever that increased my confusion, and when a woman convinced me to buy powdered milk for her baby, I let her and her accomplice rob me of all my rupees. In the alleys, butchers displayed dark red ribs, bleeding goats heads; in the little street-corner shrines, devotees left flowers and fruit to decompose. At one of the secondhand shops in Thamel, the tourist district where Western groups leave for Mount Everest or come in search of the Beatles' Kathmandu, we bought the last things we needed for the expedition: windbreakers, sweaters, boots piled up on the benches, all the stuff that trekkers give to their porters when they see them at high altitude with short-sleeve shirts and flip-flops, which the porters resell as soon as they come back down to the valley. We wandered through dust, hands, sweaty bodies, horns, and rotting garbage in the gutters, yet there was something about that city that never ceased to enchant me.

The best bars were on the rooftops, from where you appeared to rise above humanity's misery. As we talked about the journey in front of a few beers we always wound up looking north: from Kathmandu you can't see the Himalayas, only the hills and clouds that envelop the valley, but we could imagine them with trepidation. After a while, as happens in Nepal, the sensation of wasting time becomes one of adapting to a different flow of time.

It's only when you surrender that you enter the right spirit for the journey. Then, one morning, the permits to enter Dolpo arrived. We could finally leave for the mountains.

Without
Ever
Reaching
the
Summit

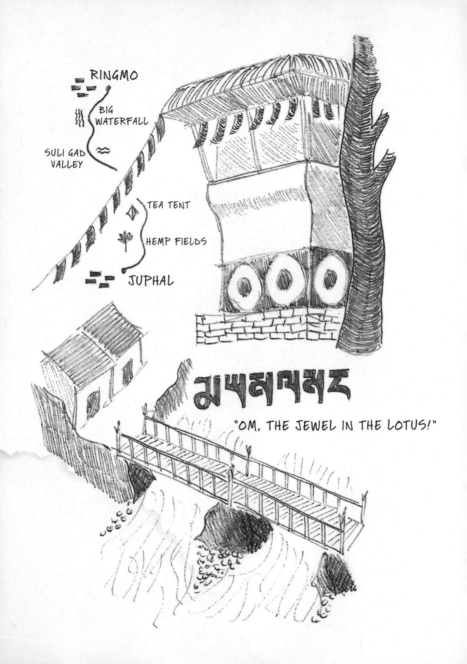

RINGMO

BIG
WATERFALL

SULI GAD
VALLEY

TEA TENT

HEMP FIELDS

JUPHAL

ཨོཾ་མ་ཎི་པདྨེ་ཧཱུྃ

"OM, THE JEWEL IN THE LOTUS!"

Along the River

On the small airplane heading north, facing the Himalayas, which emerged from the dense tropical clouds, I remembered a book received, at nine or so, from my father's hands, on a day spent home with fever. It was called *The Most Beautiful Mountains and Most Famous Climbs.* On the cover was Monte Rosa, my first and only so far. I had already tasted its rock and ice in the summer, but by winter the mountain had become a distant memory, so I spent long hours in bed with that book of color photos, to cure myself of the flu and nostalgia. I looked at the profiles of Everest, K2, and Nanga Parbat, I read about the men who had climbed them, I learned names and altitudes with the doggedness of a child for whom memorizing is a magical act that offers the illusion of possession. I dreamed of becoming a mountaineer then, reading about Messner and Bonatti as if they were Stevenson and Verne, and Tibet and Nepal were secret kingdoms, treasure islands.

Thirty years later I still knew the shape of Dhaulagiri, the westernmost of Nepal's eight-thousand-meter peaks. The airplane flew below it, grazing the puffs of clouds lit by the sun, and left it to the east. Other dark peaks emerged in front of us, a chain of them at about five thousand meters. As we had hoped, the fog stopped against that wall. Then under the propellers I began to observe sharp ridges, gorges that dropped into the morning shadows, gullies dug by landslides in the rainy season. I looked at Remigio glued to the porthole and thought I knew what he was looking for: a landscape he could read, a script he knew.

Ever since I had gone to live in the mountains, the valleys had begun to interest me more than the peaks, the inhabitants more than the climbers. I was fond of the idea that there was only one great people in the highlands of the world, but that was just romanticism; in the Alps we were now citizens of the immense European megalopolis, or of its wooded periphery. We lived, worked, moved, had relations like city dwellers. Did mountain people still exist? Was there an authentic mountain somewhere, free from the city's colonialism, its integrity intact? This was the spirit in which I had gone to Nepal a few years earlier. I had toured the most popular areas only to discover that even in the Himalayas modernity was bringing its gifts: roads, engines, telephones, electricity, industrial products, the blessed well-being desired in exchange for an ancient culture, poor and destined for extinction, just like alpine culture. I had to look harder, go farther.

The pilot whose moves I was watching veered gently, following the lines of a valley in the sun. He zeroed in on a short dirt runway, no more than a hundred meters in the middle of a slope, and lowered us for landing. We touched down and braked between the houses of Juphal, the beginning of the long trail to the north: low stone huts, terraced fields all around, almost ready for harvest that season. I still had the sweat of a sultry tropical morning on me, and as I climbed down the stairs I immediately felt the clean smell of the mountain. In the time it took to collect my rucksack the twin-engine had already taken off.

Sete was forty-seven, a Tamang from eastern Nepal. Wide cheekbones, narrow eyes, brown skin, he had been loading wicker doko baskets on his back since he was a boy. After becoming a cook and high-altitude porter, and having climbed Everest, Makalu, Cho Oyu, Dhaulagiri, and Shisha Pangma in that capacity, he too had descended into the valley with age. Now he worked summers and winters in the Monte Rosa shelters, and in the fall he worked as a guide for exploratory expeditions such as ours. He spoke Italian and laughed often.

I wondered if it was an innate joy or one of the tricks of the trade, a way to avoid direct questions. He had been in Juphal for a few days already, putting together the caravan, which consisted of him, his brother, five boys working in the camps and the kitchen, five others with animals and transport, and twenty-five mules laden with all we could use in nearly a month of walking. Plus the ten of us coming from the Alps made forty-seven animals and men. Tents, equipment, food, kerosene for cooking, mule feed, and personal baggage were loaded onto the packsaddles. The only thing we didn't bring was water: finding a stream every night and the space to camp was Sete's task; he had never been to Dolpo but had little faith in our maps. He preferred to ask muleteers and passing peasants for the way. It was hot in Juphal and I was trying to figure out what to bring in my backpack and what to load onto the mule, so I asked him when I would need heavy clothing.

"Higher up," he said.

"What do you mean by 'higher'?"

He pointed distractedly to a Y-shaped stain on the

map I had laid out, the big Phoksundo Lake lying between two valleys.

"And how long will it take to get there?"

"Four days hopefully."

"Hopefully?"

I checked the altitude of the lake: thirty-six hundred meters. At twenty-five hundred, where we were, corn was growing. Descending from Juphal to the valley floor we crossed rice fields, terraces planted with barley and millet, and lush vegetable gardens. The houses had flat earthen roofs on which hay and chili peppers dried out. Much of the life of the village seemed to take place up there, and it was all female: young women beat barley with long sticks, the old women winnowed it in the breeze that carried away the chaff; below, in a stone basin, a little girl was washing her hair with laundry soap. Elongated yellow gourds, strange peas with thorny pods, even bunches of cherry tomatoes populated that treeless slope, where only the Himalayan cedar, a conifer that had an African air to it, produced shadows between the gardens.

Looking around me, I thought of the terraces invaded by brushwood, the dry-stone walls in ruins, the irrigation canals swallowed by forests, which I used to see in the Alps. I thought about when our mountain was just as well cared for and when this one would experience abandonment. Was it a road I saw down there? Yes, there was a dirt road alongside the river and just as we reached the road we passed a small truck; a couple of years ago, as far as they told us, there was only one mule track there.

At this news I exchanged glances with Remigio. He was born in a village where until the seventies you had to climb up to it on foot; then the road came and he saw the village empty out entirely during his life. Once he told me: when the road comes it always seems made to bring things in, but then you realize it was made to take things *away*. He was watching two workers fixing the road with a shovel and pickax. I think he was reliving a scene from his childhood.

The caravan kicked up dust and the river's freshness started calling me from down below: when Sete picked a spot for setting up camp, I was the first to take off my shoes and dip my feet in the turbulent water of Bheri River. It was turbid and metal gray, from a glacier.

"Where does this water come from?" I asked.

"From the mountain."

"What mountain? Dhaulagiri?"

"Hopefully."

Sete would say "hopefully" instead of "maybe," and this gave his replies a strange oracular tone. Wherever the water came from, I had studied the maps and knew where it wound up: in the Karnali River, whose source was in Tibet; then after seven hundred kilometers it poured into the Ganges. Sitting there on a boulder, among the gnats and ferns, I told myself that my feet were soaking in the water of the sacred river.

"You've already been up there, haven't you?"

"Where?"

"On Dhaulagiri."

"Yes, that's right."

"How was it? Do you remember?"

"Long," Sete said. Then he went into the kitchen tent to supervise preparations for dinner.

I lay down to dry myself in the sun and took out the book I had brought with me from the bag. It was *The Snow Leopard* by Peter Matthiessen, published in 1978 and still on the shelves of every bookstore in Kathmandu, where worn paperbacks passed through the backpacks of new trekkers. That book also had something to do with my journey. In fact, it had partly inspired it, because I would be retracing a good section of the path described there. We were the same age, *The Snow Leopard* and I, though it may have only been a coincidence. I was now reading it for the second time.

From what I knew about him, this Matthiessen was quite likable: born in 1927 in New York, in the fifties he was part of the second generation of American expatriates in Paris, emulating Hemingway and Fitzgerald, with less luck. He also had a young wife, an apartment on the Left Bank, and notebooks to fill. Although he never produced anything memorable in France, he had been one of the founders of the historic literary magazine *Paris Review* before going back home to cultivate two passions: naturalistic studies and the exploration of the psyche. Impatient with domestic life, he soon divorced and started traveling. In the sixties he became an environmentalist and traveled far and wide in Latin America and Southeast Asia. He had explored the cultures of the natives and experimented with peyote, ayahuasca, mescaline, then a longer phase with LSD, keeping accurate accounts of his experiences. Finally, like others, he wound up dabbling in heroin. The seventies with their failed promises disappointed him, or perhaps he was his own source of disappointment, entering midlife with the realization that he had accomplished little. He grew tired of hallucinogens, became interested in Buddhist practices. He continued to write without great results.

From his point of view, it was the evolution of a quest. Then his second wife, with whom he had been on-again and off-again for some years, fell ill with brain cancer and died shortly after. Peter found himself a widower, the father of a small child, and lost in many ways. The invitation of a zoologist friend who would be going to Nepal to study the behavior of the *bharal*, the blue Himalayan sheep, came providentially. The destination of the expedition was Shey Gompa, the "Crystal Monastery" in the heart of Dolpo, where hunting was forbidden by the local lama and the wild bharal proliferated. With a little luck, their main predator might be seen, the elusive snow leopard, that "most mysterious of the great cats," which has never been observed by anyone, or almost. Wouldn't that be a good way to start over, or at least make a perfect escape? Matthiessen left his son to a couple of friends and departed. Here "was a true pilgrimage, a journey of the heart," he wrote, to "the last enclave of pure Tibetan culture left on earth." With these lines and a map drawn by hand began the diary that would bring him fame. As had happened to me before, I stumbled upon the book a little too late to know its author: Matthiessen had died in 2014, almost ninety years old, a tall, thin old man with a marked face and very light eyes. I looked at them in a black-and-white photo that I used as a bookmark and they seemed so clear to me, eyes without shadows, without secrets.

I also liked drawing maps. I would keep a journal like his, during moments of rest jotting down observations in a black notebook I had brought, strong but soft enough to fold and put in my pocket. I inaugurated it that evening. While I was finishing my notes for the day they called me for dinner: the first meal of rice and lentils in the mess tent, the first night in the little pup tent. I entered it together with the book, the pen, and the notebook, with the roar of the water that flowed by my head.

Nicola was lying in his sleeping bag next to me, an intimacy I would quickly get used to. Besides, he and I were constantly discovering surprising similarities between us: not only had we been born a few hours apart, but the same went for our fathers as well. We had both grown up in Milan (he just outside), spent some time in New York (he lived in Harlem while I lived in Brooklyn), and fled to a mountain cabin (he to Valtellina, me to Valle d'Aosta), and had never met until a year earlier, when we immediately recognized each other. We had lived parallel lives, and a dialogue in our tent could sound like this:

"Do you remember that November, the night of Obama's election?"

"Sure, I was on the Lower East Side, listening to a concert, a black trumpet player who wept as he played."

"In Harlem the women were hugging each other on the street. It was like witnessing a revolution."

"Then not much changed, though."

"But it was beautiful just to be there."

After all, I thought, *we are the Matthiessens of our times*. There was enchantment and disappointment in our New York, just like in his Paris. I had written tales of sailors while sitting on a Brooklyn pier, Nicola had started painting people walking while looking out at the Harlem avenues from his window. Later he painted the people from the mountains, more curved, always from behind, as they returned from the fields with their tools on their backs.

"Are you sleepy?"

"Not at all."

"I feel like I'm in my mountain cottage again, when the nights never end."

"But in the cottage I have grappa."

"In mine there's whiskey."

"You feel like reading me something?"

There we were, a painter and a writer. He was left-handed and I was a righty; we divided the sides of the tent, so that the good hand could take what it needed. In my case the book, the caravan's third forty-year-old. I read aloud to him: "Listen here: 'I wonder if anywhere on earth there is a river more beautiful than the upper Suli Gad in early fall. Seen through the mist, a water spirit in monumental pale gray stone is molded smooth by its mantle of white water, and higher, a ribbon waterfall, descending a cliff face from the east, strikes the wind sweeping upriver and turns to mist before striking the earth.'" After a few lines Nicola was no longer listening to me. Often Matthiessen's hallucinatory visions lulled him to sleep suddenly, so I said good night and went on reading in solitude.

Matthiessen had used a very specific word for his journey: "*gnaskor*, or 'going around places,' as pilgrimages are described in Tibet." A pilgrimage is a path of purification in every culture, but in going around places there is no point of arrival, which is fundamental for pilgrimages as we meant them. Jerusalem, Rome, Mecca: without a destination, how do we know if we have been purified? I found a connection between this need for a holy city at the end of the journey and the mountaineering obsession with mountain peaks: ever since I was a child I felt I used the summit as a metaphor for heaven, and the word "ascent" in a spiritual sense. Whereas I remembered that the most important Tibetan pilgrimage consists of going around Mount Kailash, which for that culture is sacred. *Kora* in Tibetan, "circumambulation": Christians plant crosses at the tops of mountains, Buddhists circle around them. I found violence in the first gesture, kindness in the second; a desire to conquer as opposed to embrace.

My pilgrimage began with a suspension bridge, steel cables pulled from one side of the river to the other, which led into the Suli Gad gorge, leaving the last road behind. For many days we would no longer see motor vehicles. We went up a narrow and arid valley, with the frothy stream below us and the lammergeiers circling above our heads, stopping to watch us from the cliff faces. Where the vegetation reappeared, we entered among tall plants that took me a while to recognize from the leaves. The scent was familiar. Was it possible? Hemp grew everywhere around us, very high, thick, luxuriant, near the deserted winter stables we came upon, on the land fertilized by dung. I noticed the mules grazing on it happily. I snapped a leaf off and slipped it into my breast pocket like a flower, thinking of Matthiessen and the hippie motto I'd seen on some T-shirt in Kathmandu:

NEVER
END
PEACE
AND
LOVE

"You see?" Remigio said. "They're making hay over there."

He pointed to the other side of the gorge where some women were working, bent over with small, thin sickles. The two of us had also spent hours in the fields, among mowers, tractors, balers, and trailers loaded with loose hay on which I sat while he drove. This was why the Nepalese technique interested us: here they took it away in their doko baskets, along a path that cut the slope and disappeared over a ridge. There must be a village back there, we told ourselves, and we wanted to know what it was like. We still couldn't see any men, only very small boys, little more than children: they had formed a human chain to pass a jerry can of water that the first had filled in the stream and the last would carry around to quench the mothers' thirst.

The shade of the forest welcomed us like a blessing. The hay was hung to dry on the branches of the cedars and pines, in long braids similar to lianas. On a rock wall I saw the mantra *Om Mani Padme Hum* painted, six symbols I had learned to recognize and a sound I occasionally heard being chanted: "Om, the Jewel in the Lotus!" A mysterious verse open to a thousand interpretations, which alludes to the unseen hidden within the seen. Outside there is the lotus, the form, the transient; within it, there is the jewel: the precious substance, which endures. What was hiding in those braids of hay? What was in the flight of the lammergeier, in a wild pear tree in the middle of the woods? I cut a hard and unripe fruit from it, chewed it, but it puckered my mouth and I had to spit it out. I wanted to apologize to the tree.

In the afternoon, freed from the packsaddles, and perhaps still under the effects of cannabis, the mules rolled joyfully on their backs, scratching away the burden of the load. I watched the porters and the mule drivers: they were boys of about twenty, wearing jeans and sneakers with thin soles; under the doko baskets they had curious eyes and attempts at fashionable hairstyles. They set up camp next to a small house with an outdoor table, two benches, a pile of empty bottles, a drying rack from which I intuited that the cannabis all around was a comfort the inhabitants of the valley appreciated; I preferred beer and went in to see if they had any. In the house, which looked like an emporium, or maybe it was a bit of both, a woman in broken English asked me where we were heading.

"Phoksundo," I answered, pointing at the window. "Shey Gompa. The Crystal Mountain."

"It's far," she said, holding out a bottle of beer that had a raised brand on the glass and a different one printed on the label. A Heineken that somehow had become an Everest. The woman refrained from asking the next question, which was why do we Westerners come so far to toil, sleep on the ground, suffer the cold, and be covered in dust with no apparent purpose but to turn away from our warm beds and fast cars, but I could read it in her face. If she had had the words to formulate it, would I have found the ones to answer?

At sunset, as I sipped my Everest by the river, I discovered that Matthiessen had had a similar encounter. But he had actually been asked: "I shrugged, uncomfortable," he wrote. "To say I was interested in blue sheep or snow leopards, or even in remote lamaseries, was no answer to his question, though all of that was true; to say I was making a pilgrimage seemed fatuous and vague, though in some sense that was true as well. And so I admitted that I did not know. How could I say that I wished to penetrate the secrets of the mountains in search of something still unknown?"

I put the book down and looked at Suli Gad. As the sun set, a smell of moss came down the valley along with the water. *Even without knowing what you are looking for*, I thought, *a stream is the best way forward:* it always points out the direction, you go up toward your own source, and as you see it become clearer you feel yourself becoming purer as well. I imagined the big Phoksundo Lake reflecting the glaciers from which it was born. I immersed my hand in the icy water and it seemed like a promise of that snow.

That old hippie was right. I had never seen anything like the Suli Gad valley either. I walked alone, occasionally crossing a companion, and I lost myself in the contemplation of water. Along the river the shapes struck me with such force that I often sat down to draw: Himalayan cedars, pines that looked like the Arolla pine, birch trees with yellowed leaves. A bridge made of logs stuck in the banks and jutting into the void, the posts of the railing carved by a skilled woodworker. A pile of *mani* stones, large river rocks on which mantras for the village's protection were engraved (Sete advised us to always pass to the left of such shrines, respecting the clockwise direction that governs the universe for Buddhists). Corn cobs on the roof of a house and a woman stirring fermented barley in a cauldron, from which she would make *chang*, a kind of murky beer, or *rakshi*, the raw distillate the

SULI GAD VIEWS

Nepalese imbibed to get drunk. Then puddles, rapids, shores of white gravel, islets of ferns, sandy bends. Two women riding a mule passed me while I was drawing.

I thought I heard them laughing or maybe it was a trick of the water, the mirth of a waterfall. Matthiessen: "I look about me—who is it that spoke? And who is listening? Who is this everpresent 'I' that is not me?

"The voice of a solitary bird asks the same question.

"Here in the secrets of the mountains, in the river roar, I touch my skin to see if I am real; I say my name aloud and do not answer."

Going up the stream, I came across a square-shaped tent, made of thick military green canvas, with a pair of windows and a hole at the top, from which a blackened chimney protruded. Remigio was there waiting for me. Outside the tent, a boy was splitting wood from a cedar trunk, a horse tied to a tree chased flies away with its tail, a baby with a sooty face stared at us.

"That's me when I was seven," Remigio said.

"What did you do when you were seven?"

"In the summer I would go up to the high pastures

with my mother. We had a stable and a common room where we ate and slept. In the seventies the first tourists passed by on the path. They were curious, but I was ashamed because I was always dirty, and because of the life we were living."

The boy didn't know he was facing his future self; Remigio smiled at him and he ran away. I, on the other hand, began to understand that all those mountain people were half shepherds and half merchants, so I looked into the tent to ask if we could have tea. I was right: a girl made us sit on cushions around the stove in the warm and smoky darkness and put the kettle on the fire. As we waited I looked above me and noticed strips of meat hanging to dry on a wire. From the smell I assumed it was a goat. Pots, jars, rice bags, rags, basins, and cups littered half of the tent at ground level.

"Everything on the ground, just like in my mom's kitchen," Remigio confirmed.

I put my lousy Nepalese to the test with the girl, who could have been the boy's sister, though more likely his mother. She must have been twenty years old. *Tato pani*: hot water. *Mito tsa*: good! *Didi*: girl. *Ramro didi*: beautiful girl. She smiled and poured me another cup of her black tea with powdered milk and juniper smoke.

The first snow appeared in the late afternoon at the end of a lateral valley: a peak from the Kanjiroba Himal, a chain that rises to nearly seven thousand meters, shone above the dark slopes when the sun no longer reached us. It reminded me that woods, streams, and valleys were just preludes to what was awaiting us, and my mood changed. After lingering a bit to write and draw, I was relieved to find my companions. Our row of pup tents was already set up near a village, mules grazed, and the smell of soup came out of the kitchen. I sat at a table with the others, and while they were chatting, I checked the map: it said that Sanduwa, where we were, was at 2,960 meters.

"Is everything all right?" Nicola asked me, handing me a bottle. He'd managed to get more beer, vintage Everest straight from the cellar.

"Yeah, sure," I lied.

"Tomorrow we start climbing."

"It's a pity to leave the river."

"Yeah, it was a beautiful river."

We toasted to Suli Gad by clinking the bottles. Nicola noticed something was wrong, but I didn't want to explain it to him. Anyway, there was plenty of time for him to figure it out by himself.

I never could have become a mountaineer. As a young boy I soon discovered I was susceptible to altitude sickness; my stomach was a merciless altimeter: it would start to turn on me after three thousand meters and torment me to the summit at four thousand, where I arrived foggy, often vomiting, so all the beauty of those mountains was lost on me, and what remained was just a feeling of hard-won conquest. For years I returned hoping that at a certain point the sickness would pass, but it didn't. To make up for it I started to become familiar with it. I knew when it was coming, and I learned that it would disappear if I descended. It became part of my going to the mountains, with my mind insisting, spurring, cajoling; the body obeying with difficulty and imploring me to go back, until the day when I'd had enough of that struggle and it struck me as absurd to keep fighting. Mountaineering could have remained a childhood dream. If the glacier pushed me away, there were always meadows and woods that would welcome me gladly. I hadn't climbed above three thousand meters in more than twenty years.

Not until I got to Sanduwa, where the valley forked: the village of Murwa and the last cultivated terraces to the northeast, to the northwest a deep canyon hollowed out below by the Suli Gad. I let the others go ahead and I was left alone. In front of me, beyond the canyon, there were badlands with precarious boulders balanced above high red pinnacles and jagged furrows caused by runoff in between; the water gushed from the bare earth in several places, as if it were emerging from a landslide. Which was what actually happened, the great primordial landslide from which Phoksundo was created: where the valley closed, the path became steep, climbing for the first time after days along the banks of the stream. All around, the forest that had protected me until now was reduced to dwarf cedars, thorny bushes, dog rose shrubs, dust-gray junipers.

On that slope my old altimeter kicked in again: 3,300, 3,400, 3,500 meters. My lungs felt the impoverished air, my alarmed heart began to beat too fast, my stomach contracted. I slowed down. *If I'm suffering at 3,500 meters*, I thought, *how will I get over the 5,000-meter passes?* I tried not to think about the future, the other 1,000 or 2,000 meters of altitude difference, and to concentrate on controlling my feet, legs, and lungs so that they wouldn't get into trouble, so I could keep my breath deep and regular instead of panting. I could keep my stomach down only if I stayed calm. Calm was really the key to everything, the true opposite of fear. Preoccupied with this interior work, I hardly noticed the point where, beyond me, the canyon ended and the majestic Suli Gad waterfall appeared: the water exploding halfway down the slope and falling white with foam, then flowing joyously toward the distant Ganges. I would have liked to take a bit of its lightness and soak up some of its strength for the days to come.

Finally, after passing the landslide, the path entered a hollow and eased up. Around me the sound of water vanished and pine shade reappeared. I saw new mountains on the horizon, these covered with glaciers, and pastures still green at their feet; in the pastures isolated black spots roamed, the first yaks of the journey. I spent whole summers living among the high mountain pastures in the Alps, and the grazing beasts made me feel at home. So did the soft green of the grass, the deeper green of the Himalayan pinewoods, and the gentle shapes of the peaks. Two large red-and-white chortens, similar to three-story pagodas, acted as a gateway to that world; as I passed them I came across a girl who was running. I was slow, heavy, absorbed in my controlled pace, whereas she was so light that the breeze of her run tousled her long, black shiny hair flowing over a burgundy dress and embroidered wool belt.

"*Namaste!*" I greeted her in Nepalese.

"Tashi delek!" she answered in Tibetan. From her language, the dress, those swift feet, and her Mongol features, I could see we were already over the border. The two chortens stood on a hill and as I approached the top I saw the houses of a village and, a little farther, at the bottom of the valley, the blue of Phoksundo Lake. Not the turquoise I had read about but the oil of my mood. Or was it just the sky clouding over?

Sete found us a bed by about noon. After a few nights in a tent and the prospect of who knows how many more with the Dolpo earth under our backs, it was not bad to be able to sleep on something soft and get some rest. So I spent the afternoon clearing my mind and walking around the village. But then I saw that Ringmo was more than a village; it was a real town from which caravans left for the north. Yaks, markets, and merchandise were everywhere, as were prayer flags. I looked at the square and flat houses, the stone walls, the small windows with their frames painted light blue, the piles of wood and the haystacks on the roofs. It was a language I recognized: even in the Alps the light blue of the windows keeps flies away, or at least that's what they believe, and with the coming winter, hay and wood are these highlanders' gold. In a courtyard, some carpenters worked pine trunks using primitive planes, squaring them to make construction beams. A woman sitting under a portico spun sheep's wool with automatic gestures: the spindle in the right hand turned, the left unraveled the wool, the hands moved without looking; similar to those of the monk repeating his mantra with a mala in his hand during the puja, the blessing ceremony of a new home. There were three under construction around the country. The owner of an emporium told me that they were not houses but hotels, and although the news worried me, I found them beautiful, all in wood and stone, with beams and handworked panels. New hotels were born from the woods and rocks, old chortens crumbled back into the mountain. Even the stairs that went up to the roofs were carved out of the trunks, like pirogues.

Remigio and I went to study them with the idea of building one on our return. The wind was blowing and tattered flags waved on every roof.

"Do you feel the altitude?" I asked him as we did a rough measurement of the stairs.

"I think so. I have a bit of a headache," he said. Even though he was born at eighteen hundred meters, it was the first time in his life that he had been this high.

"Remember to drink a lot. Water, tea, soup, drink even if you aren't thirsty."

"Okay."

I wanted to go and see the lake and postponed the need to lie down and sleep a while longer. Crossing a suspension bridge, I recognized a boulder Matthiessen had described, with *Om Mani Padme Hum* painted on it in the middle of the stream. I was impressed that after forty years it was still there, but the ruined monastery on the shore was maybe four hundred years old. A yak herder dozing in the bushes opened one eye as I descended toward the water. Two sensually curved Buddha eyes painted on the wall of a chorten also watched me through the trees. Which of us was watching, which was being watched?

I sat down under a juniper tree full of ripe berries and picked some of them for no reason. I put them in my pocket thinking that sooner or later I would figure out why. From where I was Phoksundo appeared endless, extending out and eventually forking between very high rock walls. According to Matthiessen, who had collected local legends from there, no fish had ever lived within it, nor had any boat skimmed its surface, which made it even more gloomy in my eyes. As much as I had always liked the swirling water of streams, motionless mountain lakes disconcerted me. I tried to make friends by sketching glimpses of her in my notebook. My line was unsteady, my hand trembled, and I had to accept that I didn't know how to draw the branch of a protruding pine that lapped the lake's surface, or the rocks emerging like archipelagos, or the ruined monastery. I focused on an idea: that the lake reflects everything, so it is made of what is reflected in it, like me at that moment. It is the only straight horizontal line in a landscape where everything is slanted, curved, broken, irregular: perhaps this was what disturbed me. Or maybe these were just distorted thoughts from the nausea that had invaded me.

I knew from Matthiessen that Tibetans believe the mountain is inhabited by spirits—not evil spirits, but nevertheless harsh with humans, and I must have met mine. "Tibetans say that obstacles in a hard journey, such as hailstones, wind, and unrelenting rains, are the work of demons, anxious to test the sincerity of the pilgrims and eliminate the fainthearted among them." I also knew that *that* demon would accompany me for the rest of the expedition, and I was willing to show him my sincerity.

It was strange to be at thirty-six hundred meters and feel like I was at the starting point, but the valley through which we had been climbing for days was suddenly forgotten; from where my eyes were I could only look up. From west to east, a crown of glaciers loomed above the basin. I had the feeling of having accessed another world: I scanned the landscape for ways to get around the lake and saw a trail carved out of the rock that went up the western shore, climbed up a promontory, then descended, or so I thought, somewhere else I couldn't see, toward Shey Gompa and the Crystal Mountain. There, where only the imagination could go, was tomorrow's way.

PORTRAITS OF PHOKSUNDO LAKE

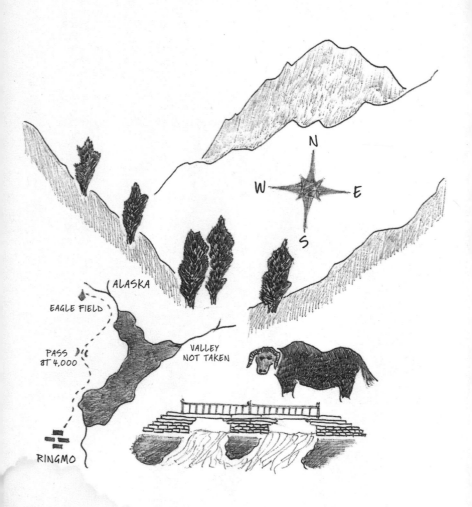

ALASKA

EAGLE FIELD

PASS
8T 4,000

VALLEY
NOT TAKEN

RINGMO

N
W   E
S

Under the Sacred Mountain

The morning when we left the lake, the caravan set off with more solemnity. The cook prepared eggs, chapatis, a last coffee; the porters loaded the dishes into the doko baskets and packed the provisions in jute sacks; the muleteers fixed the curtains and the kerosene cans to the packsaddles. They checked the knots twice, because that day losing a load would have meant it falling to the bottom of the lake. The mules snorted with some resistance, then resigned themselves and got in line behind the pack leader, decorated with a mask and a golden tassel.

The wind had subsided overnight. A damp air now hung in the basin with the promise of nothing good. Going up the promontory, we often found ourselves perched above the water, on ledges where Matthiessen had crawled on all fours or pressed himself up against the rock face. I have never suffered from fear of heights; in fact, I like to lean out and look down. Here and there the path was reinforced with stone buttresses or little bridges made of logs, and our mules, with their eyes downward, each with his snout between the tail of the one in front of him, formed a long line on the rocky side of the mountain. We climbed up to four thousand meters, where we could have jumped three hundred meters below and plunged into the lake; from up there I had a good view of Phoksundo, less the precious gem of legends than an obstacle of water that civilization had not overcome. To the south, the houses, stables, fields, and pastures of Ringmo; to the north, two branches of the lake that overlooked uninhabited glacial valleys, furrowed by meandering rivers, covered with vegetation.

Over the northwestern branch we descended through

a forest of twisted birch trees, now yellowed. Nicola said that the peeled bark of the birch trees, their tatters stirred by the breeze, reminded him of prayer flags, as if even the trees bore signs of devotion. Boulders fallen from landslides were stuck at the base of the trunks, which they had wounded and marked: the boulders, the dark scars, the whitish barks gave the woods a spectral quality that seemed to affect the lake like that morning's doleful sky.

Back on the shore we found remains of bonfires and burned trash. Timber sanded by water and carried by the current, empty cans, plastic, shoe soles. A little higher up, against a rock wall, stone shelters similar to those for goats had been built, and even there, soot blackened the stone.

"Who's been camping here?" I asked Sete.

"Tibetans," he answered.

"Tibetans from Tibet or Tibetans from Dolpo?"

He shrugged his shoulders. For him, proud Nepali that he was, they were all the same people.

"And where are they going?"

"To Shey. For religion."

"You mean they're pilgrims?"

"Hopefully," he said shortly. The word "pilgrims" didn't seem to register with him, nor did the religion in question.

A valley extended out from there on a slight slope, all gravel, birch and willow shrubs, shallow transparent streams that formed the river estuary; they branched out like capillaries, and the lake was the organ fed by the blood. Perhaps because of the pearly light and the threat of rain it seemed to me more of a northern landscape than a Himalayan one. I found the word "Alaska" on my lips and immediately afterward wondered where it had come from, since I had never been to Alaska. I would discover later that it came from Matthiessen: my thoughts had begun to blend with his in a strange feeling of déjà vu.

The northern buttresses of Kanjiroba loomed to the left as we walked away from the lake. An entire slope of the mountain was burned, so there were only stunted black trunks on that side. Tongues of grayish ice and unstable seracs stretched into the gullies almost to the level of the forest; wild yaks, distant and immobile, grazed in the band of sparse grass between the forest and the ice. Later we came across a few of them along the path and stopped to watch them closely. The cows I was used to seeing tended to stay in a herd, whereas their ancestors seemed drawn to solitude: massive, solemn, with a hump that gives them a sort of primordial melancholy, a thick dark fur made for frigid cold. Their calm, though, was only apparent. "Watch out," Remigio told me, noticing one that was eyeing me because I had unnerved him. He waved it off with a gesture I had seen him give aggressive heifers, those left in the high pastures that you come across in August. It also worked with the yaks.

We both needed a bit of free walking, so once the camp was set up we decided to go exploring. A few drops of rain were falling, and the afternoon heat brought down some seracs off Kanjiroba. Half an hour from the tents the valley narrowed; it lost the shape that made it look like a glacial slide and became a beautiful canyon, with water flowing below, between the bright yellow birches, and the reddish rock walls rising up toward the glaciers. Turning beyond a hill to look at the river,

I scared something or someone. I heard the patter of running away; the corner of my eye barely had time to notice a movement. I stepped to the side and looked through the shrubs, but all I saw were the shadows of what had already vanished.

"What was that? Did you see?"

"Too late."

"Gray rump, white tail?"

"Looks that way. Must have come down to the river to drink."

"Should we follow?"

"Not me. I'm gonna go back."

Remigio was not calm and he transmitted that uneasiness to me as well. I think it was the vastness that oppressed us. We had been walking all day without meeting anyone and we felt we were stepping into a world whose dimensions were unknown to us. He moved something with the sole of his shoe, like goat dung. I looked up at the rock walls and wondered how many presences were hidden up there watching us.

Under a waterproof tarp tied between two birches I

read about what was waiting for us. The Shey Gompa, where we were heading, was for centuries the most important monastery in Dolpo, its spiritual center. It rises at the foot of the Crystal Mountain and is a pilgrimage destination, or rather, pilgrims go there from all around the region to perform the kora ritual around the mountain, usually in the summer. The Crystal Mountain, whose summit it is forbidden to climb, is in many ways a younger sister of its most famous Tibetan brother: "Beyond the Karnali River, to the north and west, the Tibetan Plateau rises to Kailash, the holy 'Mount Sumeru' or 'Meru' of Hindus and Buddhists, home of Shiva and the center of the world; from Mount Kailas, four great rivers—the Karnali, the Indus, the Sutlej, and the Brahmaputra—flow down in a great mandala to the Indian seas," Matthiessen wrote. In this figure, the four rivers are the spokes of a wheel with the mountain as hub. Turning around the mountain by offering it your right side acknowledges its importance as a rotational axis: it is part of the wheel, the vortex of the world; the mountain is the origin of the world, just as it is the

A CANYON
NOT TAKEN

source of the rivers. Buddhism or not, I liked the fact that someone thought that way.

Whereas the Kang Pass, which we would have to go over within a couple of days, worried me. It was the gateway to Shey, and my map said it was at 5,350 meters; Matthiessen had it at 5,452. He had found it snow-covered and had gotten lost looking for the road; he had to bivouac in the cold and carry his own provisions because his porters had mutinied. In the end he crossed the pass on the last day of October, so we were two weeks ahead of him. I looked up at an altitude that I estimated at about 5,000 meters; the clouds thinned on rocks damp from the afternoon drizzle, and a veil of fresh snow melted.

God, how I missed fire! Birch branches abounded all around the camp, but to avoid uncontrolled logging, fires were forbidden throughout the region, and we, unlike the pilgrims, respected the ban. I hid under my jacket and read again, about the Tibetan myth of the *beyul*, a secret valley whose access is protected by high passes, snowstorms, and wild beasts. According to the belief, some still existed in the Himalayas: the surrounding peaks hide them from view, their slopes are impervious and battered by avalanches; but once inside, the climate becomes milder, fruit trees grow, the earth is fertile, and streams flow. They're similar to the lost valleys of alpine legends, only a beyul has nothing to do with any nostalgia for the past. Indeed, it is a hope for the future. It exists for the purpose of "giving shelter to the wise in times of violence." For this reason its secret needs to be kept, in the closed monasteries and in the silence of the lamas: it's an anti-man refuge meant to protect from wars or ecological disasters, or from any other weapon humanity might invent to destroy itself. This was also an idea I understood well. *Whoever goes to the mountains*, I thought, *must understand it.*

There was a commotion among the porters and I closed the book to see what was happening. A young eagle—impossible to confuse it with any other raptor—wound up among the mules somehow. The mules had become nervous and the porters had surrounded the eagle, but we immediately realized that it was injured: the eagle fled running on its legs; it didn't even try to spread its wings. It hid deep in a dog rose bush and stared at us, turning its head with jerks, eyes wide open.

The excitement of that encounter had already turned into pity. It didn't look so young as to have fallen from the nest, so then what could have happened? How long could a bird unable to fly survive in such a place? Soon the porters let it be and returned to their work. I was the last one still leaning over to observe it. Maybe Matthiessen was having an effect on me with his constantly delving into the unseen, but in those days I tended to see everything as a sign and wondered what a wounded eagle meant. If it was one of Shey's terrible sentinels, its agony seemed to me woefully suited to our times. Hordes of invaders weren't necessary; a fox would have been enough to execute it.

The eagle did not want my company, nor did it want to be looked at in those conditions: you can be regal even when stepping up to the gallows, in not accepting any pity. With its noble head, awkward step, claws unfit for walking, it turned its back on me and walked away into the woods, to face its destiny.

We wouldn't go below four thousand meters for a long time. I was getting used to it, but I realized that everything was more tiring for me than normal. Bending over, opening the curtain, going in, dragging my rucksack inside, this was enough to have me gasping for air, and then I had to rest a minute to catch my breath. *Is that how it feels to be old?* I thought. Forced to economize every gesture, in a body for which even the simple acts of being in the world cost effort?

Nicola came in and lay down beside me. Now with the darkness it got cold immediately and we hardly stayed with the others to chat after dinner. We drank one last cup of tea, played cards, and were in our sleeping bags no later than eight o'clock.

"Home," he said, contemplating the top of the little tent.

"This?" I asked.

"Yeah. I love it already."

"The tent?"

"It's not a tent, it's our little yellow home."

That's what happens to an artist short on oxygen, I thought. I took *The Snow Leopard* and plunged into it, leaving him to his love affair with a pup tent.

Sete sent Lakba, the leader of the muleteers, to guide us where the path became uncertain, abandoning the glacial bottom of the valley to meander, half hidden, among the gorge's rocky rises. Like all the boys in the caravan, he couldn't have been more than twenty-five. He was born in Dolpo, lived in some nearby village, and following in his footsteps I observed how he walked: distracted, in low-slung jeans and sneakers, without the commitment that we were forced to make. It didn't bother him to spend a day away from the mules, nor did he take his new leadership role seriously. Even though he didn't seem to be paying attention, he had a faster pace than ours and every now and again he sat down to look at us, strange concentrated creatures, geared up with equipment, who paid to make the effort to cross his land on foot. I would have liked to exchange a few words with him that were much simpler than these, but he didn't speak a single one in English, so I couldn't ask if he was happy (no, I would later find out from Sete: his father had just died), if there was a family waiting for him at home (yes, he already had a wife and two children), if he liked his job (at least it gave him a living: he was now the owner of the mules). Above all, I would have liked to ask him if he liked the mountain, if that mountain, which constantly moved me, aroused something in him as well, and it seemed to me as if it did as he sat on a rock in the sun, observing the distant horizon. We found ourselves next to each other, sharing that rest stop. I offered him half a bar of chocolate, which he accepted with a smile. I handed him the canteen and he drank. *How are you, Lakba? What do you think?* He smiled at me again. Then we looked at the mountains, in no hurry for the moment to pass.

Maybe Lakba was a shaman, or just watching him took the focus off listening to myself; whatever the case, the demon unexpectedly left me in peace, and in the afternoon I arrived in good shape at forty-seven hundred meters, higher than any peak I'd ever reached in my life. Up there, that rugged gorge opened up into a dry, stony basin, where trickles of water merged into the stream we had been climbing for hours. A steep terminal slope led us to the Kang Pass, somewhere above our heads, and when we turned around we were hit by the chill of Kanjiroba's immense north face: blades of bright white, seracs the color of storm clouds, high glaciers hovering— Himalaya (which indeed means "home of snow").

I felt fine, and while the others were resting I went for a walk around the basin. A pungent grass grew between the thin streams, a moss where the water stagnated, and edelweiss blossomed on the sandy ground. Edelweiss at forty-seven hundred meters! Two thousand meters higher than in the Alps. That was also the altitude for chamois and ibexes back there, and I instinctively look for them whenever I hear the sound of stones falling just above me. I looked up and saw the silhouettes of the previous day, but this time they didn't run away. There were about twenty female

SUNSET ON THE NORTH FACE OF KANJIROBA, FROM 4,700 M

bharal, or blue Himalayan sheep. For a while I had been wondering when they would show up. Matthiessen had observed them throughout his time at Shey and they had become benevolent presences on his journey, companions of solitude. They had short hair, a whitish coat with silver highlights, and a build similar to that of chamois. A single male with large curved horns was lying in the middle of the herd, staring at me like a peer. The females grazed on the grass under a waterfall, some with lambs beside them, so calm that after a slight alarm upon my arrival, they squatted down again to chew. I sat down too among the edelweiss and shared the last sun with them. I felt welcomed, accepted, not only by the blue sheep but also by the whole mountain.

I saw a caravan coming down from the Kang Pass, the first people we had run into since the lake, but more than the men I noticed the dog following them. It must have been because I missed my own dog, and it felt strange to be in the mountains without him. This dog was black, a little smaller than Lucky, and smaller than the one I had seen in other villages, half mastiffs and half shepherds, always gentle, like all the inhabitants of the Himalayas.

When I returned to the camp, I discovered that the dog was a female and that she stayed back to spend some time with us. Her fur was crusty with manure, and her teeth the white of a young animal, no more than two or three years old. She liked to run here and there and nibble on the hands we offered her. During dinner she went away, so when I went into the tent I thought she was gone, but then, in the middle of the night, we heard her barking somewhere in the camp. Nicola also had a dog at home, and from his sleeping bag he asked, "What does she hear to be barking like that?"

"Blue sheep."

"Did you see them?"

"A whole herd."

"What do they look like?"

"Like chamois. But lighter, with horns like rams. They don't run away. It must be because we're near Shey."

"What's there for them at Shey?"

"No hunting allowed."

But he wasn't thinking of the blue sheep. I heard him tossing sleeplessly in the dark.

Later he said, "I miss Macchia. Who knows how she's doing?"

"She's doing well, dreaming of you. Sleep."

"You know, she's afraid of people. She won't stay with anyone but me."

"I know."

Whereas Lucky would stay with anyone, and I was never sure if he missed me or not. The little dog barked as if she had to defend the entire camp on her own. Unable to sleep, we lay there listening to her and thinking about our dogs.

At dawn the little dog was still with us. Instead of going down the valley she followed us toward the pass, so I imagined that she had left home and was going back, and that perhaps, from there, we would find out who she was. Meanwhile, since an unnamed dog is like a lame dog, or one without a tail, Nicola and I decided to christen her for at least a day; and since we had met her under the great mountain, we immediately agreed to call her Kanjiroba. It sounded like a nice, elegant name for a Tibetan female. "Kanjiroba! Kanji!" we called out to her, so she would get used to the sound. She bounced from one to the other, indifferent to the question of the name, and a little later chased after a distant herd of blue sheep, revealing her hunting instincts.

Then in the morning I had other things to think about and lost sight of her. The climb to Kang swept away all my illusions of having acclimatized. I had a good start, I felt strong and in a good mood too, but at about five thousand meters the demon came back to haunt me. On the slope my legs began to wobble: each step cost me an effort of will and after every four or five steps I had to stop to catch my breath, except that, bent over as if searching for air on the ground, I felt like I was sucking the void. I stared at my dusty boots, and my shadow doubled over on the ground. I looked up and saw my companions, farther and farther away.

Then Lakba caught up to me, and as he passed me he understood how I was doing. *Follow me*, he said in silence. *All right*, I replied. I followed him step by step, keeping my eyes on his feet and entrusting myself to his rhythm, slow but steady, a rhythm measured specifically to pull me up. Did he want to thank me for the chocolate from the day before? Or had we established a friendship at that moment, sitting together watching the mountains? Under the hill I saw him bend down to pick up a stone, and I imitated him. After so much effort, the fearsome Kang Pass turned out to be only a harmless gap full of rocks. Up there, among the frayed prayer flags, Lakba placed his stone on a pile of similar stones. *"Ki ki, so so,"* he murmured. I knew that mantra: *ki* is the cry of the eagle, and the wind, *so,* is the deep breath of the earth; the pass is the point where the spirits of the wind and the earth collide with each other, and as we arrived up there we brought a gift to placate them, so they would let us through. I also placed my stone on the cairn, but without saying anything. Lakba had already returned to look after the mules.

Downhill my legs felt free, happy to lose altitude and gain oxygen in the blood. I practically started running. This was how Shey appeared to me after a couple of hours of new lightness: a valley of pastures, still green in October and at forty-two hundred meters. It was at the confluence of two streams. One that Matthiessen called the Black River, tumultuous and full of water, which I had just descended along from the south, and the placid White River, which joined it from the east. At the bottom of the valley, on this side of the bridge, two shepherd's tents were pitched and a few yak calves wandered about, but I saw from the large stone enclosures, from the divots on the ground just how much traffic that summer pasture got. Beyond the bridge, on a rise facing south, the monastery buildings stood out in the sun. The gompa's dominant position, the red of the walls, and the flags waving on the roofs gave it the appearance of a fortress.

As I passed by one of the tents, I found Kanjiroba playing with a girl of about ten, while a child of three or four toddled behind them. Both wore a maroon tunic and belt with colored stripes, and had beautiful Tibetan features on faces soiled with earth and soot. The mother was sitting outside the tent, spinning yak wool. There were six small prayer mills near the Black River, but the canal feeding them was dry: in autumn there wasn't enough water to spin the wheels inside the mills, cylinders on which the mantra *Om Mani Padme Hum* was inscribed. I wanted to see them in the spring. I liked the idea that it was the stream praying, with the cattle grazing and the children playing, oblivious.

I passed the bridge and climbed toward the gompa, composed of an imposing Tibetan stupa, some houses that looked uninhabited, the monastery itself, and a large square field behind it covering an area of about ten meters per side. Closed off by high stone walls, it looked like one of our cemeteries. There was no one around: neither monks, nor pilgrims, nor shepherds. I put off exploring it until later; I would have plenty of time to go around, and that last little climb reminded my legs of the Kang ordeal. I took off my rucksack, lay down on the meadow, and soon fell asleep in the sun.

We stopped at Shey for two days, during which I filled my notebook with drawings and notes. Matthiessen had spent twenty days at Shey watching the blue sheep and following the snow leopard's tracks, visiting the nearby hermitages, questioning the monks he met. The leopard had never shown up, but just waiting for it had given him meaning, as if standing still waiting for something were a form of meditation. He had placed a small earthenware Buddha outside the tent. He would sit there every morning at dawn, "happy and sad in the dim instinct that these mountains are my home." The word "home," the nostalgia of some ill-defined place, appeared for the first time in his pages. He also wrote of his Buddhist practice in those days: "Homegoing is the purpose of my practice." At times he thought of his son, which reminded him that it was almost Christmas in the distant world. He had to figure out where home was.

There was something miraculous about raising my eyes from his diary and finding one by one the things described by him. Forty years for Shey had passed in the blink of an eye. No discoveries and inventions, no wars, revolutions, youth movements, no collapses of empires and ideologies, no music and literature: nothing that had happened in the course of my life had left a mark there. The strange terrain behind the gompa was not a cemetery, but the largest cairn field that Matthiessen had ever seen: the walls themselves, sixty paces each, were made of stones from those cairns. I climbed to get a look inside and saw that the field was covered with them, and the gray-blue stones, broad and flat, smoothed by rivers and carried by pilgrims for centuries, formed piles taller than a man. On many was inscribed the mantra *Om Mani Padme Hum*, sometimes in a design similar to the petals of a flower. *Must be a lotus*, I thought. Om, the Jewel in the Lotus!

I was trying to count the stones when I heard the same mantra murmured by a monk who, rather than scolding me, just smiled at me happily. I jumped down from the wall to greet him, but he couldn't stop and motioned for me to follow him. He was making his round, his afternoon kora around the prayer field: with his left hand he was counting on a mala and with his right hand he was whirling a prayer wheel, a cylinder with a handle similar to a *damaru*, or prayer drum. Following behind him I passed among the red houses, some with the roof collapsed, leaning against each other above the monastery, without seeing signs of life from the windows and courtyards. Frayed fabrics fluttered on every wall, and a flock of wild pigeons drew

THE GREAT STUPA OF SHEY

wide turns in the sky, respecting the clockwise direction we were moving in as well.

I followed the monk to the entrance of the gompa: in front of the closed door was a bed of blankets, and he placed the prayer wheel next to it, but he held the mala in his hand. *If he sleeps outdoors,* I thought, *on the threshold of the monastery, he must be a sort of guardian.* He didn't respond to the two or three words with which I attempted a conversation. But he looked at my silver earrings with interest, and his attracted me: coral and turquoise, the precious stones of Tibet, fixed to a metal post in his earlobe. *Do you like them?* I asked with gestures. *Let's swap.* He smiled again, showing ivory teeth and the fine lines of a cheerful man, marked only by age and sun.

When I got back to the camp I found it full of activity: while my companions drank tea, the porters washed each other's hair. They drew water from the stream, warmed it on the kerosene stove, and poured it over each other's soapy heads. They didn't seem to suffer from the cold or the fatigue of the day. They looked like they were preparing to go out for the evening. Then they smoked, and I saw one do a mock dance with the others, laughing, a cigarette between his lips, swaying his hips to an imaginary rhythm, until Sete summoned them to order and sent them to peel potatoes.

I took out a special flask I had put in my bag and sat outside the tent to enjoy the last sun. Down in the valley a caravan arrived with wood, square beams similar to those I had seen in Ringmo. Maybe those yaks came from there; *if they went west*, I thought, *they were probably headed for the border*. In the past, the salt of Tibet was transported over this same route, to be traded for tea and rice from the Indian plains; now tea and rice came from China, but Nepalese wood was still precious in the highlands. Each yak carried two beams that the caravaners were unloading for the night. They were tired men, covered in dust, with the cantankerous ways of those who work with cattle. Kanjiroba barked at the yaks heading for the fences, and this was the only sound that came to me, delayed by the distance, multiplied by the echo.

What was the source of the harmony I clearly perceived in that landscape? Maybe it was in the proportions among the mountains, or in the two rivers that joined in front of me to become a single river? I realized that the valley was a kind of sundial: the White River marked the east, the Black River the south, and the river they formed together was the west. So at dawn and dusk the sun aligned itself with the valley, and along the way it turned around the Crystal Mountain. As for the mountain itself, it did not seem any different from the others: a trapezoid of reddish rock against the darkening sky.

"Why is the Crystal Mountain sacred?" I asked Sete, who for once seemed to be enjoying a moment of rest.

"Because from the summit you can see Kailash."

"What do you mean?"

"That's what they say."

"But isn't it forbidden to go up there?"

"Yes, because it's sacred."

I looked at him and he looked back at me like a foolish student. It seemed like one of those puzzles on which Buddhist practitioners meditate, to overcome rational understanding and access an intuitive one. The koan Sete had assigned me sounded like this:

> *Who has seen Mount Kailash*
> *from the untouched summit*
> *of the Crystal Mountain?*

I decided to drink on it. Nicola came to sit beside us and said, "It would be perfect now if we could have a drink."

"You're telling me."

"Try this."

I handed him the special flask: it was Scotch whiskey aged and peated, which I had safeguarded so I could open it at Shey. He uncapped it and a whiff was enough to lift his eyes skyward. He went to get two cups from the kitchen tent, poured the whiskey, and added a drop of Himalayan water to the nectar of Scotland. It's hard to imagine ever tasting a better drink in my life.

In the morning the two rivers were veiled with ice, the wood caravan had left. A woman was gathering yak dung and throwing it against the walls; when the patties dried and fell off they were ready to burn. I wanted to visit a hermitage not far away and together with Nicola and Remigio took the path that went to the west, going up in altitude as the valley turned rugged and its slopes grew steeper. After the last ridge, Tsakang appeared in front of us: four stone buildings perched on a ledge overlooking the river. Even the last stretch of the path was gouged into the rock and it seemed crazy to imagine living on such a precipice, but for the Tibetans this was precisely what gave the hermitage value: its nearness to the wind, its position in the full sun, the tumult of the water below, the Crystal Mountain's "white pyramid sails on the sky" in the clear morning. Then as we approached we saw that even that narrow cornice had been patiently worked, tearing tiny cultivated terraces out of the rock.

"Potatoes," Remigio said. He had been eating mountain potatoes all his life. "Soon they'll dig them out."

I gave a spin to a prayer wheel, which creaked in a niche in the wall. Nearby I discovered a small woodshed of juniper roots and a larger deposit of yak dung. These are the two fuels of the hermitage: the fire was lit with wood and fed with dung. Following a small black tube that ran along the gardens, I climbed the terrace system to a cavity in the rock wall, too shallow to be called a cave, just deep enough to enter and squat. The rock was damp inside, and on the bottom of the cavity, I found not quite a spring, but a pool of water gathered from the dripping wall. Next to it were a ladle, a bucket, a miniature earthenware Buddha, and offerings of faded flowers, which made the cave look like a small shrine, and the pool a holy font. Then I remembered the juniper berries I had picked up on the shore of Phoksundo. I thought of that boundless lake and the minuscule one in front of me now.

I still had the berries in my pocket: I fished them out and arranged them along the edge of the pool, near the withered flowers. Then I dipped two fingers in the water and wet my eyelids and lips, which were burned by the sun in those days. At night I licked them; they felt strange under my tongue, but I didn't have a mirror to see how chapped they were, whereas my eyes were fine. As I wet them I thought, *Let me know how to look and let me find the words to tell what I saw.*

"Someone's coming," Nicola said. A man and a woman were going up to Tsakang along a path different from ours. The older woman wore a bundle of juniper roots tied with string on her back. The man was a round-faced monk, with a red robe and shaved head, who invited us to follow him to one of the buildings. We entered through the little wooden door, then climbed up a ladder to the vestibule between two rooms: a bare kitchen, with a stove in the center and a few shelves on the walls, and a prayer room full of colored fabrics, pillows, candles, holy books crammed on very old wooden shelves. A butter lamp illuminated a photo of the Dalai Lama torn from some newspaper. *Come, come*, the monk nodded to us; *sit, sit down.*

He showed us how to cross our legs and how to join our thumb and middle finger, sat down between a large suspended drum and the window open over the precipice, and put a sheepskin on his shoulders. Then he began reciting. I have never been uncomfortable with the prayers of others. In fact, they give me great calm. Remigio stayed outside. I looked at Nicola, who nodded and smiled at me. I closed my eyes to concentrate on the monk's murmuring and could distinguish the smells of incense, of leather, of yak butter burning in the lamp, of the mountain coming in through the window. Withered grasses, the night's humidity evaporating, the rock warmed by the sun, the morning. Even in an ancient place like that, the mountain always smelled new. "In another life—this isn't what I know, but how I feel—these mountains were my home," Matthiessen had written. "There is a rising of forgotten knowledge, like a spring from hidden aquifers under the earth."

The sound of a drum made me open my eyes, an

echo that started some internal membrane vibrating in me. The monk produced a series of beats, he used a curved iron with a leather ball attached to the end—*bum, bum, bum*—and with every beat my belly resounded, and then the ritual ended. There was an offering box next to the Dalai Lama's photo and we were happy to leave our rupees there.

In the kitchen the woman had turned on the stove and was boiling water for tea. She prepared it the Tibetan way, with salt and yak butter. In a bowl she kneaded the *tsampa*—toasted barley flour and water—and that would be their morning meal. I looked at the monk, who made a ball of dough with his fingers and dipped it into the tea like a biscuit, and I remembered the scene in which Matthiessen, in that same hermitage, had asked the lama of that time the most difficult question of all. The lama, crippled by arthritis that deformed him and imprisoned him up there forever, burst out laughing and raised his arms to the sky as he replied, "Of course I am happy here! It's wonderful! *Especially* when I have no choice!"

Neither Matthiessen nor I could understand such an answer. No more than we knew who has seen Kailash from the Crystal Mountain, or what the sound of one hand clapping is. After making tea, the woman let the stove go out. But I was so attracted to the fire and missed it so much in those days that I asked her with gestures for permission to feed it with one of her precious juniper roots. They didn't need it for anything, and yet she nodded. I laid the root on the embers and watched it burn while they drank tea.

In the afternoon I did my laundry down at the stream and laid it out in the sun. I asked Sete to wash my hair, and I washed the rest of me with a basin of warm water, then put on some fresh clothes. My companions also freshened up. They stretched out some rope between one tent and another and hung the laundry to dry. Only when I walked away, and I turned to look at the field, did I notice the comic sacrilege: our underwear flapped on the laundry cords; prayer flags stirred on the roofs, walls, and wooden poles. But Buddhists appreciate irony, and no one would be offended at Shey. Inspired by the scene, I thought how in the realm of the wind, those faded and ragged fabrics had the specific purpose of venerating it. The wind would not be seen if there was nothing to wave: the flags make the invisible visible. The vultures that hovered with open and immobile wings were priests of the air.

I was wandering among the prayer wheels when the girl from the day before came with Kanjiroba in tow. She wanted to show me something in secret, and stretched out her hand and opened it: it was a shell fossil, a reminder of the time when the Himalayas were at the bottom of the sea. India, which was then an immense wandering island, had run aground against China, the mountains had risen in the impact, and the shells wound up at four thousand meters. I shook my head no. I didn't like the fossil market or the child merchants. The girl was a bit upset. I had chocolate somewhere and offered it to comfort her. She turned to the tent, I think to check if the person who sent her was watching, then grabbed the chocolate and ran away.

I sat down against one of the mills and watched the monastery. Higher up, on the grassy slopes of Mount Somdo, a herd of bharals grazed in the sun. No leopard in sight, but the afternoon sky was clear and at that altitude the light had something absolute to it, like light in its purest state. The same with the rarefied air I breathed, the icy water I caressed with my hand, the rock warmed by the sun against which I was sitting. That purity corresponded to the purity within me; this was the thought I was trying to shape: the wind, the stream, the light, the stone were of the same substance as my blood, my fibers, my organs, and resonated with them like the monk's drum had shaken my membranes. *Bum, bum, bum*: I am made of this, of this, of this. The mountain led me to the essence.

Matthiessen had focused on the same feeling in the most poignant pages of his diary. All I basically did was rewrite what he had written at the time, and yet it seemed to me completely appropriate at Shey: there nothing went forward or backward but turned in circles, following the motion of eternal return, or eternal rewriting. And it was no idle movement. For the Tibetans the spinning of the wheels, our going around walls, monasteries, and mountains, activate the prayers inscribed inside them just as the clapper that caresses the edge of the bell makes it vibrate and produce a note. In Kathmandu I had heard the F of Tibetan singing bowls, able to make water dance and skip when filled. *If this is true,* I thought, *then from Shey one powerful note must expand into the universe*: the pilgrims wandered around the Crystal Mountain; the smiling monk circled around his monastery; the mills fed by the streams turned along with the flock of wild pigeons that revealed, perhaps, a granary hidden in the gompa; writers turned around the meaning of their being there. Who has seen Mount Kailash from the untouched summit of the Crystal Mountain? I closed my notebook. At the same time, but forty years earlier,

Matthiessen closed his, in which he had written, "The secret of the mountain is that the mountains simply exist, as I do myself: the mountains exist simply, which I do not. The mountains have no 'meaning,' they *are* meaning; the mountains *are*. The sun is round. I ring with life, and the mountains ring, and when I can hear it, there is a ringing that we share."

Matthiessen finally decided to part with his zoologist friend and rejoin his son before Christmas. A few days after his departure, his friend had finally caught sight of the snow leopard.

"It's strange," Nicola said as we were getting our rucksacks ready. "Leaving a place is knowing you'll never see it again in your life."

I had a still stranger feeling, that I'd be coming back, but I thought it would sound too sentimental and kept it to myself.

The girl, seeing that we were leaving, had gone up to the camp to watch us roll up the tents with a betrayed air about her: *What do you mean, we've just become friends and you're already abandoning me?* Kanjiroba, who had been hanging around her all the time, looked undecided between two instincts. Then, as we started to go, her doubts evaporated and she followed us. "No, no," I told her. "Stay here." But it's quite impossible to change a dog's mind once it has decided to follow you, unless you're able to treat it very badly. So twenty-two human beings, twenty-five mules, and a little dog set off again. She was the forty-eighth of the caravan.

It was a long good-bye because, going up the gentle White River valley to the east, Shey remained in sight for hours. Sometimes I turned around to remember it better. I was afraid of the Saldang Pass, only slightly lower than the Kang, but as I climbed, I realized that the two-day break had done me good. On the last slope I even managed to enjoy my heart beating, my lungs pumping air, and I couldn't imagine the landscape awaiting us there. It was a moment: the last steps up-hill, the cairn of votive stones, the prayer rags, then the view opened wide over the desert of high mountains.

The border between Nepal and Tibet was somewhere in front of my eyes: between rows of brown, smooth, sandy peaks, slopes of yellowish grasses and patches of dull red shrubs, sparse snow. The snow formed domes suspended over those very arid hills, higher than six thousand meters. In the valleys the icy beds of the torrents glistened and lines of sand went up the slopes to the ridges: the cattle tracks. After days of walking, I understood that a whole new journey began from here.

I was on the pass musing over the plateau when on the other side a caravan of yaks laden with goods came in a din of hooves, cowbells, and shouts. A boy chased an unruly calf, hurling insults and stones at him as he struggled to bring him back to the herd. An old man at the tail end stopped to ask us something; he pointed to his eyes, swollen and reddened by ophthalmia, and obediently allowed me to put in the eyedrops we offered him. Grateful for the relief, with tears streaming down his dusty cheeks, he pointed behind me and asked, "Shey Gompa?"

"Saldang!" I said, pointing behind him.

The old man nodded. He felt my thick beard from the West and caressed his own sparse whiskers from the East, then shook his head as if to say that he was the old man, he should be entitled to the more beautiful beard.

That's too bad, I thought. I would have given him eyedrops, rupees, chocolate, whatever he wanted, but never my beard in exchange for his.

"*Ki ki, so so*," the old man said, then headed behind the beasts in the dust.

SALDANG

NAMGUNG

DHO TARAP

Through a Border Valley

The place where we camped that day looked like a ghost village. It had been built at a strange position, right at the mouth of a gorge, from where the stream that had dug out that canyon gushed; so during the floods the water had stolen land from the houses, it had reached their walls and was eroding their foundations, which seemed to be the reason they had been abandoned. Yet the fields had recently been mowed, the dung was spread out on a slope in the sun to dry. Where had everyone gone? I followed a disused irrigation channel, an engineering project where the water would flow over arches spanning gaps and cracks; I found two entrance chortens to the village, a wall of mani stones, rusty prayer wheels, and a dilapidated gompa. In Namgung even the religion had a neglected air, a devotion to old cults no one believed in anymore.

The first inhabitant to show up was a girl who ran down from the pastures, crossed a small bridge, and disappeared in the courtyard of a house. Shortly afterward an old man came out to check who was there, and while I tried to communicate with him I saw that behind him, in the shadows, the girl was carrying a child on her back. She wore it wrapped up against her as if they were one. The old man looked at me suspiciously: only after a series of polite pantomimes, with me pointing at the gompa, did he reluctantly take a large key hanging by the door. He led me down an alley and pushed away a sort of overlay of brambles from a wall. As soon as I got past it I discovered the reason for his suspicion: all the barley from the harvest was there, in the courtyard of the monastery, blond sheaves arranged in long ordered rows. A flock of pigeons also circled around that gompa and I couldn't believe it was a coincidence.

I remember the autumnal *désarpa* of the mountain herders around my parts, the descent into the valley with the cattle at the end of the summer pasture season. Probably even in Dolpo the inhabitants left the high villages to winter at lower altitudes once the harvest was over. We were at forty-four hundred meters in late October; there would be snow soon. Inside, the monastery contained peeling frescoes and monstrous masks, but now it served more as a granary than anything else. All that remained to protect the precious barley were the wild pigeons, the bramble fences, the dusty sacredness of that building, and an old guardian. And yet, what better fate for a temple no longer in use?

Kanjiroba had become familiar with us and now she wasn't just hanging around. In the morning she would burst into the tent. At six o'clock the porters shouted, "Coffee!" and gave us sahibs the luxury of serving it to us in our sleeping bags. This was how we woke up from our restless nights, Nicola and me: with moka coffee and the cheer of a stray dog.

"I already put sugar in," I said while she jumped on us.

"Why always to us?" he complained.

"Eh, who knows why?"

Some in the caravan had begun to think that Kanjiroba was the reincarnation of a sinner monk, forced into this other existence to roam the highlands. To me, though, an animal did not strike me as an inferior life form to that of a human. On the contrary: who could have lived free in those mountains if not a griffon vulture, a blue sheep, a snow leopard, or a dog?

So a suspicion came to me, and after Nicola left the tent I looked into her eyes. *It's you, isn't it? Wasn't it you who wrote*, "To glimpse one's own true nature is a kind of homegoing"? The dates coincided: Matthiessen had died in 2014 and Kanji could have been three years old. For the Tibetans, no more than fifty days pass between one existence and the next. This is the period in which we wander through that kingdom of the dead called the *bardo*—and then we're off on another spin of the merry-go-round. *So is that what happened, Peter?* The dog didn't answer. I scratched her nose and she licked my hand with the contagious affection of dogs just waking up: they greet you every morning as if they haven't seen you in a lifetime. *Well,* I told her, *you really figured out a nice way to get home.* Then I got out of my sleeping bag, all rumpled and damp from the night's condensation, and spread it out in the early sun.

By the time we got down to Saldang, at thirty-nine hundred meters, I was beginning to lose count of the days walking. It was the closest point to the Chinese border that we would touch throughout the journey. Tibet was there, about twenty kilometers away, beyond the passes that closed off the valley. I was expecting another remote village; instead we found a small town nestled in the valley of the Nagaon River, with scattered settlements surrounded by fields and grazing cattle. The women were busy in the courtyards: flails threshing the barley to a synced rhythm, wicker sieves scattering bran in the wind.

But other signs hit my eyes after days in the mountains. I had already experienced it in the Alps: the purity that we attain, or have the illusion of attaining as we rise to an elemental altitude, is quickly tainted when returning among men, and with it the clarity of thought becomes muddied. Saldang confused me with its satellite discs and solar panels, plastic litter everywhere, and the national flag on a roof. Not since Kathmandu had I seen the rhododendron flower waving. Then a soldier came out and I understood: we were at the barracks of a border town, as there are soldiers at all the world's borders.

I wanted to explore streets and alleys. Sete rented a courtyard for us to set up camp and asked the lady of the house if she could make us tea. On the front door I saw the reversed swastika of the Bön religion engraved, a shamanism prior to Buddhism that had survived for centuries, half hidden, in some Dolpo villages. Inside, I passed by a mirror that I carefully avoided looking at. The stove was in the center of the room, on the bare beaten earth, and the woman invited us to sit on simple rugs and pillows. It was the first time we had entered a house, and while waiting for tea I looked around trying to imagine the life of those who lived there.

The wall in front of me was completely occupied by a rack of wood, pine or cedar, dark with soot, and burnished by use. Among the crockery, bags of rice and tea, photographs of weddings, the bright colors of the freeze-dried spaghetti bags and canned drinks stood out. A fake Coca-Cola, a fake Red Bull, all the marks I had seen among the garbage along the path. The photos of the Dalai Lama were among those of the family as if he were an uncle, a member of the household. Only when I turned around did I notice the poster looming behind me on the rough plaster of that little wood-and-stone house, a print almost as wide as the whole wall.

It was a vision of Lhasa in the future, when the Tibetan capital could hardly be recognized among skyscrapers, highways, parking lots, and shopping centers. It looked like a Los Angeles in the mountains. Whoever had imagined it at least had the heart to leave Potala, the ancient royal palace, even though it was hidden by towers and junctions. That was the place from which the Dalai Lama had fled in 1959, when the Chinese army cracked down on the revolt of his people. From then on he was a king in exile. It was impossible to ask the woman if she understood the difference between the two Tibets, and which one she desired. The propaganda poster's provenance, like the noodles and Coca-Cola, wasn't hard to guess: Nepal was far away, its streets not less than a week of walking, whereas great China was just behind a row of mountains.

I had no right to feel nostalgia for the poverty of others, but I was upset when I stepped outside again. Sitting in the courtyard was a drunk old man praying. He did it his own way: he gave his prayer wheel a turn, recited the mantra, poured himself a cup of liquor, threw it down, then continued praying. I observed the wide riverbed, the slopes eroded by water, the crumbling chortens meant to protect villages and fields. In that same landscape, forty years earlier, Matthiessen had seen the decline of a civilization. But he was not a good prophet when he wrote of Saldang, "One day human beings will despair of grinding out subsistence on high cold plateaus, and the last of an old Tibetan culture will blow away among the stones and ruins." He was wrong. Famines would not kill them off: those mountain people have always faced hunger. So I corrected him: "Sooner or later these human beings will build a direct road to China, from here trucks full of goods and illegal immigrants will pass, barracks of all kinds will rise along the valley, and the riverbed will be reduced to a landfill; and the last vestiges of an ancient Tibetan culture will disappear amid garbage and cell phones."

Om Mani Padme Hum, the old man muttered. Om, the Jewel in the Lotus! I would have liked to ask him for a sip of his liquor.

It must have been three in the morning when I heard Kanjiroba whimpering like beaten dogs do and I suddenly sat up from my sleep.

"I'll go," I said even before Nicola realized what was happening.

I freed myself of the sleeping bag, grabbed a boot to use as a weapon, and stepped out of the tent, shining a light with my headlamp. The scene I saw shortly after snuffed out all my aggressive intentions. Maybe it was because of the rage I'd accumulated toward Saldang, but I had misinterpreted those noises and felt like a father looking for his daughter late at night, only to surprise her at the door with someone.

"What is it?" Nicola asked as I came back in.

"Kanji's found a lover," I answered.

"Well, well. And you sent him away?"

"She'll send him away if she wants."

We said to ourselves: *this time she'll abandon us and start a family in Saldang. Farewell, Peter, you lucent soul!* Instead we turned into forty-nine the next day, and later into fifty. We went up the river and in each village Kanji attracted a dog that followed us for an hour or two. Then, reluctantly, her suitors returned home, and she kept going straight. She seemed to know exactly where she wanted to go.

Now we were heading southeast, back toward the

Himalayas. We walked between villages and fields, exchanging *tashi deleks* with women and sharing the path with children going to school. They had worn-out briefcases, dusty blue uniforms, bottles of milk tea for breakfast, and they laughed with us as they tried out their textbook English. In Namdo they all entered a large courtyard filled with rows of desks and two blackboards hanging from a wall. Before the lesson they lined up in blocks, the males separated from the females, and sang a song, which I assumed to be the national anthem, in front of teachers as strict as army officers. When they broke ranks, the soldiers returned to being children: the bigger ones ran to their desks, the little ones to play. One of the teachers threw stones at a yak calf that had entered the courtyard to look around. A short distance from the walls of that open-air school ran the shimmering river; above the students' heads the sandy mountains burned in the sun. It looked like a valley where it had never rained and would never rain. We hadn't seen a cloud or a tree or a flower for days.

In an emporium I bought a fabric with blue, yellow,

red, white, and amaranth horizontal stripes, then tied it to my rucksack. I did it for no reason; it was just my way of expressing how I couldn't stand borders. One of my teachers said that borders are particularly odious in the mountains, because on both sides of the watershed the same grain is cultivated, the same beasts graze, they have the same customs; so if there's a border it should be between mountains and cities, not between mountains and mountains. With that cloth draped around me, I noticed that the peasant women were pointing at me to each other and they greeted me amusedly.

"Buddhist?" one of the barley threshers asked.

"No, pacifist," I said, but I don't know if she understood. She smiled all the same. In the evening I attached the cloth to a stick and planted it where we pitched camp, thereby making it our flag.

That night I finished *The Snow Leopard* for the second time. I felt so good immersed in that book that I immediately missed it. Nicola was asleep, so I had no one to communicate that feeling to, the kind of sadness that only readers know, the nostalgia for finished books. Our nights fit well together, like the space in the tent: he fell asleep immediately and toward one or two began to turn over in his sleeping bag, whereas I didn't shut my eyes until midnight, but then with a little luck went straight on until dawn. I listened to the sounds outside. There was the stream flowing and my pacifist flag flapping, plus another sound that took some time to recognize. It was the typical work of a dog gnawing on a very large bone, blocking it with its paws, digging its teeth in to wrest the cartilage and little filaments, for hours and hours. Who knew what Kanjiroba had found?

I reopened *The Snow Leopard* to the first page, to the Rilke quote: "This is at bottom the only courage that is demanded of us: to have courage for the most strange, the most singular and the most inexplicable that we may encounter."

And then, like someone knocking at the door of an old friend, I turned the page and started over again.

———————

Kanjiroba had found a bharal's head. In the morning she was still trying to tear something from its sockets, from the scraps of skin that remained attached to its skull. We were now far from the villages, inside the river's gorge, near the water; judging by the state of that head, blue sheep had been grazing around there until a couple of days earlier. Now it was just food, and it triggered in Kanji a voracity that I didn't feel like watching.

After leaving the course of the Nagaon we no longer ran into anyone. The vegetation of thorny bushes made it difficult to leave the path, so we had all kinds of tracks at our feet. "Look," Remigio said when we were over four thousand meters again. He was the son of a hunter and in the mountains he always read the tracks of wild animals for me. He showed me a row of them with a stick: the big palm, the four round and splayed fingerpads, the whole footprint measuring about half a man's hand. I placed mine next to it to compare. It wasn't a wolf, or a dog, or a fox. It was certainly not a blue sheep or a Tibetan antelope. It was a cat, and at that altitude we knew there was only one.

"Not only is it rare," Matthiessen wrote, "but it is wary and elusive to a magical degree and so well camouflaged in the places it chooses to lie that one can stare straight at it from yards away and fail to see it. . . . The snow leopard is the most mysterious of the great cats; of its social system, there is nothing known. Almost always it is seen alone; it may meet over a kill, as tigers do, or it may be unsociable and solitary, like the true leopard."

The one that preceded us was a loner: the row of footprints indicated an easy, regular pace that went down to the stream, then came back. Since the ground was still frozen at eight o'clock in the morning, they must have been left the night before. So the blue sheep's head came to mind, along with a question I hadn't asked myself: who had killed it? I looked up at the barren slopes, at the labyrinth of valleys that branched over my head, certain that somewhere the snow leopard was watching us.

Reflecting on that day, it seemed to me that the elusive character, the talent of being there without showing oneself, belonged not only to him but also to the whole land of Dolpo. We only encountered signs of things that had happened, missed by just a little, fleeting, like those traces of flour accompanying us for a stretch of the path, which made me think of a punctured bag on the back of a mule. Or the deep burrow in the reddish earth that brought to light a network of underground tunnels.

"They extract marmots from here," Remigio said.

"What do you mean, 'extract'?"

"They hunt them when they're in hibernation. In the winter they gather deep in the lair to keep warm, in a sort of central room, you see? If you find them with a pickax you'll kill them all."

"Why?"

"To eat them, no?"

"Have you ever?"

"I've heard about it."

Leopards, men, and the times eluded us. At forty-five hundred meters we reached a plateau you could see must have been a summer pasture. Up there in October, the perimeter walls of two tents remained—squares of four meters per side—and it was like looking into a house whose roof had been removed: the hearth in the center; the beaten earth all around; the stone niches on one side, which served as pantries. Not far from the tents, the yak pen. As I walked around in the pasture, I found a goat skin that was hardened and fibery, a porter's belt, a sachet of powdered broth, a hammer and sickle drawn on a stone. Right there, another elusive footprint. That little symbol in yellow paint looked even older than the pens and hearths, which seemed to have no age, whereas this did; it went back to the time of the Maoist insurrection in the Nepalese valleys in the late 1990s. A tiny relic of the twentieth century. A negligible dream of revolution on the periphery of the world.

"Have you ever?" they will ask us one day.

"I've heard about it," we'll answer.

We returned to the twenty-first century, descending toward the next village, where we were greeted by a large inscription composed of white stones on the mountainside. WELCOME, it said, next to a chorten repainted in bright colors. The welcome had to be for us and for the other tourists who would arrive, or so we hoped, since at the moment there was no trace of anyone. Entering the village, we passed the Himalaya Hotel and the Dhaulagiri Hotel, both of which were deserted. They were simple one-story buildings, a dusty courtyard, a low wall around them, not unlike the other houses. On the flat roof wood was drying for the winter. The dirt road ran between the river and this single row of buildings, and as we followed it a man on a mule passed us: it was Lakba, my silent guide. He spurred with his heels and quickly disappeared, kicking up dust.

"Where is he going?" I asked Sete.

"To his uncle, to tell him we're coming."

"So this is Lakba's village?"

"That's right."

"What's it called?"

"It's called Dho, on the Tarap River."

I remembered the day we had left. Lakba and his mules were waiting for us at the small airport. The airplane, Juphal, the cannabis fields seemed so far away to me: starting from Dho, even taking the shorter route, they must have spent days coming to pick us up.

A little later we saw a motorcycle approaching. It had polished chrome and two speakers blasting Indian pop music. The rider looked like his bike, with a leather jacket and sunglasses and some kind of gel in his hair. He passed us slowly, checking us out; if he wanted to impress us he certainly succeeded. When he left I asked Sete how a motorcycle had arrived in Dho. He told me that they brought them in from China, taking them apart and loading them onto mules.

"And then where do they go?" I asked.

"Nowhere. Where the village ends, so does the road."

We saw more of those bikes parked outside a tent next to a ruined gompa. The tent must have replaced it, because inside there were some twenty monks celebrating a ritual. Seated on the ground, with prayer books in front of and cups of tea beside them, they chanted to a rhythm kept with plates and drums. They were almost all young, little more than boys.

Others—older and more elegant men, perhaps the owners of the motorcycles—attended the ceremony without paying attention to us passing by.

That evening, from Lakba's uncle's house, I watched the crows circling over a hill. We discovered that we had run into a funeral and that they still practiced sky burial in Dolpo. Wood was too scarce up there for cremations, so the corpses were dismembered and transported, in pieces, to a height where the birds of prey could complete the process. For Buddhists, the body is made up of elements borrowed from the universe, and once life leaves it, they must be returned; the matter in which we have lived returns to its state of air, water, and earth, and is recirculated through the birds. I wasn't wrong at Shey: they were the real priests.

I saw a girl who opened a fence and led her sheep to graze across the river. The sheep jostled each other on a narrow wooden walkway; the lambs wound up in the water and trudged across the shallow river.

To celebrate the return of his nephew, Lakba's uncle had a pot of rakshi boiling in a shed in the courtyard. Only one of us was brave enough to ask for a cup: me.

"What does it taste like?" Nicola asked.

"Hot gasoline," I answered.

"That's the taste of methanol," Remigio said. "Don't bother."

We settled for a safer imported Lhasa Beer, the Tibetan version of Everest, and we went to the little party. The porters and the muleteers were cheerful and boisterous; they had already started on the barley beer. They wound up getting drunk and late in the evening got into a fight with the local boys. There was a coming and going of motorcycles all night long. Lakba's uncle became angry and we heard him go outside, shouting. In the morning we would find them ashamed and bruised, heads down as they secured the packs on the mules.

I'd had enough of the valley and its air of death. I couldn't wait to go back to the mountains.

In the Desert

I must have still needed to be purified of some sins or to prove my sincerity, because while climbing to Jhyarkoi Pass the altitude demon tested me harder than he had until then. When I felt him arrive, Dho was already a thousand meters and four hours' walk lower. I was climbing so well throughout the whole morning that I deluded myself into thinking that I had been accepted by that world, welcomed as a creature of the high plateau. But then, on the final rise, he attacked my stomach, where the torment had begun. *There you are*, I thought as I felt the twinge. *Were you waiting for me?*

I looked up and calculated that I had another three hundred meters of ascent above my head, a long and monotonous sandy path. I slowed the pace: one foot after the other, the heel of the advancing foot no farther than the tip of what would follow, and at the same time the breath. Right, inhale; left, exhale; one foot after another. I had to stare at the ground in front of me, concentrate on my breath, and not look up toward the hill; otherwise the agony would have been worse. I told myself that with this rhythm I could stop at every bend in the path; it would have been no more than thirty steps at a time, but then I found myself stopping every twenty, and then every ten. One minute to gasp for oxygen every ten small steps.

It wasn't enough for the demon, and an icy wind began to blow on me. My hands and feet tingled. *This is the blood flowing poorly*, I thought, *or the head losing its grip.* I no longer felt my fingers and pulled my feet up like there were two rocks tied to the ankles, someone else's feet. I realized that I was dragging them. *Can you at least stop blowing this wind?* Now I bent down to look for air every three or four steps, protecting my mouth and nose with my arm. *Enough wind, please. Please, let me through. Ki ki, so so.*

My body slowed under the weight; it kept responding worse to what I asked it to do. One part of the head was my will, the other confusion. I was foggy when I found myself sitting against the stone heap on the pass, at fifty-three hundred meters, unable to speak. Nicola was next to me and I could see that he was exhausted too. All I could think of was walking down the other side, but this time losing altitude didn't give me back my lucidity: I'd be lying on the ground one minute, tripping over my feet downhill the next. My feet were no longer mine. Then I was lying in a tent. Who knows how I got there, or what time it was? I was shaking in my sleeping bag. I couldn't get the cold of that wind out of my bones.

Remigio called me from outside: "*Paolín*, come near the fire." That name was something between us and all I could do was follow my friend's voice.

It was dark outside. They had really lit a fire, there were shadows of porters around a big juniper burning, but I immediately realized that getting out of the sleeping bag was a mistake. The chills increased. From Remigio's tent, hanging above the entrance, I saw a bharal skull staring at me. "It's the shaman's tent," he said, grinning, the bonfire blazing in his eyes. Flames, shadows, skulls, my friend had gone mad from the altitude. I felt like I was inside one of Matthiessen's dreams, in one of his hallucinations.

Someone handed me a bowl of soup but as soon as I smelled it I knew I couldn't eat it. I took a canteen of hot tea, went back into the sleeping bag with all my clothes on, and curled up. *But what am I doing here? Why am I shaking at five thousand meters, nothing but frozen darkness all around and my stomach twisting? Why am I not at home with the woman I love, dinner on the table, some music, a warm bed? What is this damned call of the mountain?*

Instead of drinking it, I took the tea canteen and held it against my belly in the sleeping bag. It turned out to be a good idea. After a while my stomach calmed and the chills stopped. I felt a warm welcome, sleep came over me, and the demon finally left me in peace.

The next day I cured myself with a long walk on a slight slope, hours and hours in a valley without houses or men. There was nothing to look at but the desert, the cloudless sky of Dolpo, the frozen streams that slowly melted in the sun. The water up there stopped every night and started flowing again every morning. From a height I could see the entire caravan, scattered for miles along the valley: my companions walked at a distance, meditatively. We were tired and maybe we were entering that phase of the journey where you begin to count the days left and start imagining your return. That sense of leaving increases the fatigue, takes away the taste for discovery.

Remigio kept his mouth and nose hidden in a scarf throughout the morning. I walked up to him and asked, "Did you really put a skull on the tent, or did I dream it?"

"It was to pick up your spirits," he said. "Do you feel better?"

"Yeah. I'm a little weak. And you?"

"I have a sore throat. But my legs are working."

I had fragmented memories of the evening, and now I was trying to put them back together like a drunk the morning after a binge. Above all, I felt I owed a debt to my friends. Who had waited for me on the hill? Who had taken my rucksack and unrolled my sleeping bag? Who had made me tea? At one point someone looked at me, gave me two pills, told me to stay warm and drink a lot.

I went to Nicola and asked, "How's it going?"

"Better than yesterday. I had a little fever."

"Did you get any sleep?"

"Hardly. But you sure slept. Feel better now?"

"Like new. Were you the one who put me to bed?"

"Yeah. Don't you remember?"

"No. But thanks."

In a valley we came upon a frozen pond. With his stick, Nicola drew a leopard, a wolf, and a crow on the ice. All he needed was a few strokes; he had a talent for simplicity. They weren't randomly chosen figures: those three animals bound us, they were at the origin of our friendship and our journey, and we watched them shine on the ice lit by the sun.

After a while, in the valley, which neither rose nor fell, two boys on horseback appeared as silent as spirits. They had long, straight, black hair, scarlet bands on their foreheads, coral and turquoise earrings. Even the horses were decorated, with gold tassels, colored ribbons tied to the tails, embroidered blankets under the saddle. They seemed to be going to or coming back from some ceremony. From the way they rode there was the naturalness of nomadic peoples, and I couldn't imagine a more just and harmonious way of crossing the desert. They barely looked at us as they slipped away in the opposite direction. I watched them withdraw, farther and farther until they disappeared into the plateau's shapes.

The village from which those riders came looked like a village of dust. It was perched on a hill at the confluence of two streams, and something about it, set there high above the water, reminded me of the citadels back home. I knew that at one time the Tibetans had been marauders on horseback, they had come down from the north to raid these peasant villages, so maybe I read Charka's need to defend itself correctly. But now the wind was kicking up clouds of sand, and the sand had the same color as the houses, and it was like seeing the houses erode and crumble. In the dust, a girl came back from the pasture with goats while black ravens with wings outspread watched us from midair.

It was impossible to pitch tents outdoors, so Sete rented a house for the night. I felt grateful for the sleeping board, the woolen blanket, the smoky warmth of the room where they set us all up together. I tried salted yak butter tea for the first time—nauseating if you thought you were drinking tea, good and refreshing if you thought you were drinking broth. The little family that hosted us spent the evening in a small room behind a curtain, perhaps a small kitchen: a man, a child, and a young woman speaking good English who came every so often to see if we needed anything. When they went out to sleep somewhere else I got up to stretch my legs, looked at the books on a shelf, and succumbed to the temptation to look around: next to the stove dying out, the pile of dry dung, the tsampa bowl, two butter lamps flickering in front of a photo of the Dalai Lama. Above the photo hung a Tibetan flag. Gifts of wildflowers, ears of barley, even rupees had been brought to the picture of the Dalai Lama, smiling. I immediately withdrew with the shame of an interloper.

In the morning the woman came back alone. She went into the kitchen and soon the juniper smoke enveloped us. In Dolpo I hadn't been able to talk to anyone, and I doubted I would get another chance. So while my companions were drinking coffee, I went to the tent and knocked on the doorjamb.

"Can I come in?"

"Please," the woman said.

I went in. She was kneeling in front of the stove and

blowing on the fire, which wouldn't catch. I remembered reading how many children in the region had eye and throat problems because of the smoke.

"Is there anything you need?" she asked.

"Only to talk a little, if you want."

"But of course."

I sat down on a stool next to the stove. I noticed that the butter lights were out on the small altar. The woman caught me looking there but was not at all embarrassed. She had a natural elegance as she shut the stove door, adjusted her skirt, and sat down too.

"How come you speak English so well?"

"I'm a teacher. I learned in Kathmandu."

"You grew up there?"

"I went to school there. I still go back every winter. It's too cold here, there's too much snow to stay. But this is my village, I wanted to teach the children here."

"Is it far, Kathmandu?"

She thought about it, counted with her fingers, and said, "Four days walking to Jomsom. Then another two or three with the bus or a ride. A week."

"And when do you leave?"

"In a little while. Everyone is gone by December."

Morning light filtered through a window. Outside the wind had not stopped blowing all night. Now it was keeping the stove from catching, and the sun played with the puffs of smoke between us in the kitchen. I pointed to the photo and the lamps and asked if she could explain their meaning.

"We are Tibetans," she said. "Our language, culture, religion. But we are Nepalese citizens and very grateful to Nepal for letting us live our way." In this refined response, I thought I heard the speeches she gave to children. Then she added, "It was my grandmother who came here from Tibet and married my grandfather. I still have many relatives there."

"Do you go see them?"

"I can't. The border is opened only a few times a year. So we meet at a mountain pass three days from here, to say hello and exchange gifts."

"In Saldang?"

"A little closer."

Four days walking to catch a bus, three to greet her family. It took us twelve hours by plane to go from Europe to Nepal, but now that I was sharing those spaces, walking for three days seemed totally normal to me too.

The woman filled a kettle with water from a jerry can and placed it on the stove. The fire struggled to stay lit, so much so that I doubted it would ever be able to boil that water.

"Listen," I said, "can I ask you a question? Ever since we left I've been wondering. I wanted to know what all of you think of us passing through."

"You're a great help!" she said, putting her hand to her heart. She was afraid she'd offended me somehow. She said, "Everyone would like to rent a room out to people like you. Come back to see us. Come back!"

I thanked her. I believed her, but I had too many doubts to take that answer at face value. I told her that we might never come back, but I was sure that many others would come in our place. I smiled at her.

"How many children in your school?"

"Fifteen."

"Are they good kids?"

"Yes, very."

I left Charka, village of dust, feeling as if I had merely grazed it. Taking down the camp every day is the law of the caravan, but to understand a place you need to stay. We walked away with the low smoke that couldn't rise above the huts, the strong smell of juniper that would stay in our clothes for days. I hadn't even asked her name.

And yet it was so beautiful, so instinctive and necessary to get back on the road. Leave the known world behind and continually discover a new piece of the world. Walking was our daily mission, our measure of time and space. It was our way of thinking, of being together, of getting through the day, it was the work our bodies now did on their own. Although thinned, bruised, and feverish, each morning they stood up and trudged meekly like mules. Walking reduced life to the essentials: food, sleep, encounters, thoughts. No invention of our age helped with anything as we walked, except for a good pair of shoes and, in my case, a book in my rucksack. For weeks I lived on rice, lentils, vegetables, sometimes eggs and cheese, my copy of *The Snow Leopard*, my notebook, my friends. Even more than being able to make do with so little, it was surprising to realize that I had no desire for anything else. Only when we stopped did the need arise, the nostalgia, the aspirations, all the emptiness to fill.

I hadn't thought of Kanjiroba in a while—she was an autonomous presence by now, no one cared about where she slept or what she did when she wasn't there—but after a stretch of path along the river I saw her on the other shore: a black dog running and trying to join us in vain. The bridge we had crossed was much farther back and she was afraid of those suspended walkways, so now she was looking for a point where she could wade across the wide, fast, still partly frozen river. She didn't trust the current. She tested the depth with her paw then pulled back, tried another way, and whimpered. Nicola and I approached to call her. "Kanji! Come! C'mon, you can do it!" Then she jumped in with the blind trust of dogs: she slipped on an icy boulder, fell into the river, disappeared in a rapid, and emerged a little farther down the valley, gasping. Finally she found a foothold. It was so cold that in no time her water-soaked coat whitened with ice. She shook it off and ran cheerfully into our arms.

Walking that day, and thinking of the woman from Charka, something occurred to me that I had forgotten to do, and that I had to do before the end if everything was to be done right. I stayed back, waited for our porters, and said I wanted a photograph of everyone to remember them. The boys were very proud of it: one by one, they took their loads off their backs and posed. After taking the photo, I gave my notebook to each and asked them to write their names, and I still have them in black on white, names with different and halting penmanship: Suren, Sangeh, Subash, Kailas, Darma. One was shy, one showed off his muscles, arms folded, one smiled next to his basket. The cook, the camp hands, the one who went to draw water from the river and then wash the dishes. He was the last of them all, Darma, small and scrawny. He carried the stove in his basket and you could tell he was approaching from the smell of kerosene. I had the feeling that he was isolated from the others because of some difference in caste, his darker skin. *Me too?* he seemed to ask me when I handed him the notebook. *Yes, of course, you too*, I replied, nodding.

We were walking steadily above forty-five hundred meters, in a landscape I no longer noticed: burnished, arid, sandy, the same for days. The gaze of those who cross the desert is directed within. We went up and down, we gained a hundred or two hundred meters and then we lost them again. That was all we had done for weeks; according to my calculations we must have walked for three hundred kilometers as the crow flies, but the unevenness of those endless ups and downs was incalculable, as was the true length of the path. I thought that the Himalayas, like Sete, rebelled against our measurements. I realized already that saying "gain" and "lose" reflected an economic sense of going to the mountains that was entirely Western, where altitude and distance are the capital we accumulate with our effort, and we would not like to squander our investment for any reason. I seemed to hear Matthiessen's voice: *Change your words*, he told me. *Change how you think.* Who has seen Mount Kailash from the untouched summit of the Crystal Mountain? Look for the answer in these ups and downs: because you will lose everything you thought you had gained; learn that the path is much more precious than the summit. Find a meaning in every step. Within this concentration.

In the afternoon the river widened, separating into streams and rivulets, and became a marsh. Many of the pebbles I trod on were fossils of shells. On that high altitude seabed I noticed a movement beside me. I turned around; it was a hare: a beautiful gray hare in an alert position, ears perked, muscles tense and ready. What was a hare doing up there in late autumn? We stared at each other for a moment, before Kanjiroba arrived. Then the dog set off in pursuit and the hare fled up a slope so fast that it disappeared in a few bounds. *Here is the fourth animal guide*, I thought: *a leopard, a wolf, a crow, a hare.*

We set up camp at just under five thousand meters. The next day the last pass was waiting for us, the highest of all, above fifty-five hundred meters. I wasn't sick but it was very cold and as soon as the sun went down behind the mountains the torrents started to freeze again. I thought that it must be many degrees below zero for the ice to form in front of your eyes. When I picked up my stuff to bring it into the tent I found something under my rucksack: it was a jar of strawberry jam, new, sealed, like the one we ate for breakfast. Could it have fallen from some porter's basket? Strange that it wound up right under my rucksack. It occurred to me that someone had put it there. I looked around. I soon met other eyes that were waiting for mine: from afar, facing the kitchen entrance, little Darma was watching me. I tried to smile at him and took refuge in the tent.

Later I read aloud, "With the wind and cold, a restlessness has come, and I find myself hoarding my last chocolate for the journey back across the mountains—forever getting-ready-for-life instead of living it each day. . . . Exciting days have occurred since their arrival, and yet a kind of power is winding down, a spell is broken.

"And so I, too, prepare to go, though I try hard to remain. The part of me that is bothered by the unopened letters in my rucksack, that longs to see my children, to drink wine, make love, be clean and comfortable again—that part is already facing south, over the mountains."

"Drink wine, make love," Nicola said.

"Are those your wishes for your fortieth birthday?" I asked, putting the *Leopard* away. Lately I kept it in my sleeping bag along with my notebook and tea, because outside the paper would get soaked with frost. It was the condensation that froze against the cloth of the tent, and if at night one of us moved too much our frozen breath would fall on us.

"I don't know," Nicola said. "How many wishes do I get?"

"Three," I answered.

"In that case, I want to paint. I want lots of kids around me. And I want a woman who's happy with her life."

"No more tormented girls?"

"That's right. No more."

"I still like them," I said.

I touched my nose, the only part of me sticking out from the sleeping bag. It was already starting to become a foreign body. My mustache was always damp; later in the night it would be frozen too. I pressed the tea canteen against my stomach.

"And then?" Nicola asked.

"I want to write. And a lot of mountains all around."

"You haven't had enough of mountains?"

"For now, yeah. But you know what happens: as soon as we get down I'll want to go back up."

We stayed silent. I could hear the voices of the porters in the kitchen tent. *Who knows what they're say-*

ing? I thought. I thought of Darma, who had been in there drying the dinner dishes. Once the work was finished, they also pushed stoves and pots into a corner and lay down to sleep, but first they spent some time smoking and chatting. With these voices that I didn't understand to keep me company, my friend a few yards away, the few things I was attached to with me in my sleeping bag, I already knew how the Dolpo nostalgia would be. *One last shot over five thousand,* I thought. Then I told myself to stop with all those thoughts; otherwise I wouldn't be able to sleep anymore.

In the morning all I did was put on my boots and leave the tent. In the beginning we wanted to change clothes, to wash ourselves; now I wore the same clothes for days and, if I could, I would have kept my shoes on in my sleeping bag. Brushing my teeth down the stream was all that remained of my personal hygiene. At seven Kanjiroba was white with frost, curled up at the edge of the field and waiting for the sun. The mules grazed on the grass burned by the frost, the stream crackled: the ice on the surface thinned and broke, then fell into the water and was carried away by the current. The thawed water between my lips woke me up completely.

During the climb I asked Remigio to tell me about the fire three nights before. I couldn't swallow the fact that I'd missed it. He was a good storyteller, and I liked listening to him; even at home we often shared the trail that way.

"It was Kanzah, Sete's brother, who lit the fire," he said. "Do you remember how cold it was that day?"

"Sure, I remember."

"Even the porters were cold. As soon as they saw the fire they all gathered around."

"And you with them?"

"First I went around collecting wood. What little there was, dry twigs, some roots. I thought, *You don't go to someone else's fire without bringing a little wood.*"

"Seems right. Is that how you do it in the mountains?"

"I don't know, that's what I thought."

"Can I write that phrase?"

"Write whatever you want."

"And then?"

"It was nice because there were no more differences between us around the fire. It must have lasted half an hour in all. I stretched out my hands with them and thought, *Ah, fire!* Then I saw that the little guy had his palms all cut up from the basket strap."

"Who, Darma?"

"Is that his name? I went to get him some bandages and put them on his wounds. He was all happy."

"That's why you came calling me."

"Yeah, but you were too sick."

Along the path he thought about what else to tell me, and after a while he added, "Do you know the biggest difference between the mountains I remember and these?"

"What's that?"

"They smile. I remember my mother and aunt when the first tourists came through. I remember them closed off, they didn't say hello to anyone. Here they're always smiling."

"You're saying they're more hospitable?"

"Or happier. At home there was a lot of anger; here I haven't seen any. But I don't know if I saw right."

The climb was gentle and the air still, the sun warm. It was tiring but I didn't suffer getting to the pass. Up there, at fifty-five hundred meters, the northern face of Dhaulagiri appeared before us: a hundred kilometers of glaciers, ridges, spurs, peaks higher than seven thousand, up to the main one breaking eight thousand. From where we were it seemed impossible that someone had imagined climbing it.

On the other side of that chain there was Nepal, changing rapidly, a small country squeezed between India and China, more and more reduced to the periphery of the others; and on this side, "fallen behind history," as Matthiessen wrote, were Dolpo and us. The ragged flags sent prayers to the wind. Wherever one might turn, there were no other signs of human presence.

I stayed up there for a while enjoying the midday sun. As I lay on the hill I was letting my heart and lungs slow when I heard female voices next to me. The laughter of girls—is there a happier sound in the world? I opened my eyes: there were three of them, climbing up a slope that was breathtaking from the top, but they chatted among themselves and, putting down their baskets, adjusted their hair and skirts as if after a short run. They looked at me; you could see that I amused them. My pacifist flag triggered hilarity since I had hung it on my rucksack. One of them spoke to me, pointing to her lips but I didn't understand what she was asking—a word? lip balm? a kiss? *They are hungry*, I thought, and I willingly gave them my lunch: a boiled egg, a chapati, a piece of yak cheese. Although weak, I had no appetite because of the altitude and I couldn't stand another egg. One of the girls accepted my surprise gift and split it with her friends. *Thank you*, she said with a nod. *Thank* you, I replied.

We shared that last stretch of path with carpenters from Charka, two men and a woman loaded with tools and who would bivouac at night not far from our camp. We slept in tents, they in the shepherds' stone shelters.

We used sleeping bags designed for twenty degrees below zero, they wrapped themselves in woolen blankets. In the three days it took us to descend from the plateau we passed a ridge that seemed to me only another fold of the mountain, but for them it must have had a special meaning: they stopped beside a cairn, put down their baskets, and lit a juniper fire. The wood was green and made more smoke than flames; the pungent smoke that by then I knew well would forever remind me of Dolpo. The carpenters passed through it, stopped in the smoke, raised it with their hands, breathed it, reciting the mantra *Om Mani Padme Hum!* Om, the Jewel in the Lotus! The smoke seemed to be some kind of threshold. After their passage the juniper continued to burn and so we crossed it too. "*So, so, so,*" Sete murmured. "*So, so,* rock 'n' roll" was our cook's version, anticipating the party he was going to throw back in the city.

Many of us used our phones to take pictures and charged them with small solar panels, but by now we had forgotten what their original function was.

There was no signal on the plateau, but in the valley floor toward which we descended there was, and as soon as we got over another ridge my companions' packs began emitting a flurry of sounds. We looked at each other as they received the messages accumulated in a month of silence. Messages, emails, notifications, missed calls. *Welcome back to the desert of the real*, I thought. We were back in the net, in the world, in time, and I could feel that timeless world—the monk's tea in the hermitage overlooking the abyss, the tattered and dog-eared *Snow Leopard* in my rucksack—already losing its meaning. Who has seen Mount Kailash from the untouched summit of the Crystal Mountain? Now my koan was just a good phrase for a T-shirt in the Kathmandu stalls.

"The fine lunar clarity of life at Shey swiftly diminishes," Matthiessen noted along his return journey. But shortly afterward he recognized the need for loss. "Even transparency, O Pilgrim, may be a hindrance if one clings to it. One must not linger on the Crystal Mountain."

THE TREE WHERE DOLPO ENDS

The last of the thresholds was a tree, a dusty and wrinkled Himalayan cedar. I hadn't seen any since Phoksundo Lake, and it struck me so that I stopped to draw it. While I was painting it I noticed that clouds had sprung up above the cedar, behind Dhaulagiri. Clouds! Clouds and trees were linked. I turned toward the slope behind me, a rise of a thousand meters and more leading back to the high plateau. I had already noticed the grassy bluffs where the blue sheep grazed. The blue sheep were Dolpo's sentinels, the cedar and the clouds its last threshold. And up there, somewhere, was the snow leopard, to remind me that not everything that exists is visible to the eyes, not everything is understandable, not everything can be gathered and taken with you. "And in the not-seeing, I am content," Matthiessen wrote. I was leaving something unseen and untouched behind, but I had come so close as to feel its presence. That's what you feel coming down from the mountain. Then I closed my notebook and passed under the cedar's branches, down into the valley.

Kanjiroba disappeared in Kagbeni, the town at the

entry to Mustang, where we arrived in early November. Mustang is well frequented but the trekking season was ending and the town's small hotels were almost all empty, from the makeshift hovels to the beautiful wooden guesthouses, all with a slight hippie vibe from the Nepal of the past, like the one we splurged on for our first night in a bed.

Under the shower I burst out laughing with pure joy: laughed and laughed and laughed at the hot water flowing over me and how my body, recovering sensitivity, was still able to feel pleasure. Now that we were back under three thousand meters I was hungry and thirsty, and that evening I would interrupt my vegetarian diet for a two-finger-thick yak steak, roasted mountain potatoes, a bottle of Australian red wine, and a deep, long sleep finally for many hours.

But before dinner I went for a walk and realized that Kanjiroba wasn't there; she wasn't curled up at the threshold of our guesthouse, she didn't come out of some courtyard or alley as she always did in the villages. Kagbeni isn't a city, it's a smattering of messy houses; passing between them are bicycles, flocks of sheep, stray dogs, off-road vehicles over the muddy unpaved roads, as well as porters and caravan mules. I bought a beer in an emporium and went to drink it near the bridge over the river. On the other side of the bridge was the path we had descended, on this side the ramshackle town, and under the bridge the river that came from Mustang, the great Kali Gandaki. To the south it passed between Dhaulagiri and Annapurna as if between two immense pillars, and in Kagbeni they must have assigned it some sacred attribute because right next to the bridge I saw a pyre. There a corpse had been burning for some time, and the pyrekeepers swept the ashes toward the river. In Nepal, around the cremations, there are no women in tears, no processions of men dressed in black, no signs of mourning or pain, only life that carries on, the bikes, the stalls, the people talking, so much so that even I with my beer wasn't out of place there on the bridge. The ashes of the corpse fell into the Kali Gandaki and went down with the current; it was matter returning to its cycle,

DAWN ON THE PRAYER MILLS AND
ON THE CRYSTAL MOUNTAIN

returning to the water, to the earth, to the air through the fire. Within fifty days the vital breath that had inhabited that body would reappear in another form, maybe a child, a bird, or, who knows, even a puppy.

I looked at every stray dog passing through the streets of the town, one by one. In half an hour I went around the whole town, but nothing—Kanjiroba wasn't there. She wasn't with our porters camped in a courtyard, nor among the packs of black dogs rummaging in the garbage, nor in the company of some male in an alley. *Peter*, I said, *where are you? Did you go back? Have you already taken the path back to Shey? Are you already running home? Forty years*, I thought. My friends were waiting for me, and I told myself that my life too would be starting again soon. Then I made my way back to the bridge and finished watching that lifeless body burn.

Acknowledgments

Fontane, 2018

Thank you to Adriano and Fausta, in love with Nepal. To Luca, Pierluigi, Beatrice, Patrizio, traveling companions. To Stefano and Remigio because our friendship always takes us a little further. To Sete, Lakba, Kanzah, Suren, Sangeh, Subash, Kailas, and Darma: it was an honor to share the path with you.

My support to Sanonani and CASANepal, to the children and women of Kathmandu.

This book is for Double-Bottle Nic, for the drawings still to come, and in memory of our master Tiziano, who led us to the Himalayas.

Tashi delek